ANOINTED
DESTINY CHANGING PRAYERS

FOR YOUR CHILDREN

A PRAYER TOPIC A DAY

TABLE OF CONTENT

TITLES   **PAGES**

Objectives Of The Parent Interceding Ministry

Oh Lord, Give My Children Glorious Beginning

My Firstborn, Receive Divine Release

Oh Lord, Open Book Of Remembrance For My Children

Oh Lord, Launch My Children Into Seasons Of New Things

Oh Lord, Deliver My Children

It's Time For My Children To Rise And Shine

My Children Must Prosper

Oh Lord, Bless My Children

Oh Lord, Remember My Children For Good

My Children Shall Receive Divine Visitation

Heaven of My Children, Open

Oh Lord, Fight For My Children

The Glory of My Children Must Shine

Oh Lord, Position And Promote My Children For Their Next Level

My Children Shall Break forth And Breakthrough In Life

Oh Lord, Raise Divine Helpers For My Children

TITLES	PAGES

My Children Will Reach Their Goal

O Lord, Perfect Everything That Concerns My Children

Blood Of Jesus, Speak For My Children

My Children Will Excel In Life

My Children Must Succeed

Name of Jesus, Speak For My Children

My Joy Over My Children Shall Be Full

My Children Will Fulfill Their Destiny

The Story Of My Children Will Change

Oh God, Give My Children New Song

Oh Lord, Favour My Children

Mercy of God, Speak For My Children

OBJECTIVES OF THE PARENT INTERCEDING MINISTRY

Parents Interceding Ministry was established by divine inspiration and express approval of the General Overseer of Mountain of Fire and Miracles Ministries, as a Ministry within the MFM Ministries in September 2006.

The Objective of the Ministry in the main is to gather all parent together, once a month, to devote quality time to pray for and pray out problems, unfavourable situations, delay and denial affecting our children, young and old.

There is no doubt that many children are passing through silent problems such as:

- unemployment
- lateness in marriage
- delay in having fruit of the womb
- physical and spiritual sicknesses
- witchcraft attacks
- prolonged pregnancy
- miscarriages
- broken marriages
- activity of strange woman
- attack by spirit husband/wife
- mental illness
- attack of the brain, resulting in poor academic performance
- widowhood and attendant problems
- in-law attack

- foundational problems
- effect of polygamous contamination
- wrong marriage
- evil companion
- cultism
- sexual promiscuity
- business failure
- project stagnation
- bedwetting
- physical disabilities.

The list is limitless but the power of prayer is able to subdue them all.

"Jan 5;16... The effectual fervent prayer of a righteous man/woman availeth much"

It is gratifying to report that God is moving and many wonderful testimonies are been recorded every month to the glory of God.

Parent Interceding Ministry is essentially a praying one and free. All it costs you is your presence and active participation. You may come with the photographs of your children if you so desire.

The meeting holds every last Saturday of the month at the Main Auditorium of MFM International HQ from 12:00noon prompt.

As you come, God will bless your efforts, change the story of your children, give them new names and put a new song in their mouth.

Remain blessed in Christ Jesus!!!

1 OH LORD, GIVE MY CHILDREN GLORIOUS BEGINNING

Praise Worship

Scripture Reading: Isaiah 45:1-3

Confession: Rev. 21:5

PRAYER POINTS

1. I raise the altar of God in prayer against any power refusing my children having a glorious beginning this year, in the name of Jesus.

2. Every power of darkness holding the souls of my children captive against a glorious beginning, this year, die, in the name of Jesus.

3. Every foundational strongman and stronghold binding my children to Satan, release them an die, in the name of Jesus.

4. Oh Lord, let every altar of family idols working against a glorious beginning for my children, catch fire and burn to ashes, in the name of Jesus.

5. Every evil security watching over the progress of my children this year, thunder fire of God, blindfold them, in the name of Jesus.

6. Every evil water, river or fountain assigned to trouble the glorious beginning of my children, dry up from your source, in the name of Jesus.

7. My children shall not be casualty of evil this year. Any diviner assigned to pronounce destruction against my children, carry your evil load and die, in the name of Jesus.

8. Every to and fro progress designed for my children this year, die, in the name of Jesus.

9. Every power of limitation, anointing of stagnation and demoting spirit operating in the lives of my children, die, in the name of Jesus.

10. O Lord baptize my children with grace and glorious encounter in this year, in the name of Jesus.

11. O Lord as my children begin this year with you, give them a new and glorious beginning, in the name of Jesus.

12. Every satanic agent on assignment to block the glorious beginning of my children this year, somersault, confess, run mad and die, in the name of Jesus.

13. In this year, the miracle that is difficult for others to receive shall be a daily occurrence for my children, in the name of Jesus.

14. The height that others cannot reach is where people will find all my children shining as the stars, in the name of Jesus.

15. This year, O Lord, let the lives of my children be separated from failure, hardship, poverty, lack and sickness, in the name of Jesus.

16. This year will be a year of celebration and jubilation for my children, in the name of Jesus.

17. You my children, in this year, leap into your breakthroughs and glorious beginning, in the name of Jesus.

18. My Father, test my children with goodness that will push them into a glorious beginning this year, in the name of Jesus.

19. Power source of any problem programmed to embarrass my children this year, dry up and die, in the name of Jesus.

20. Every power assigned to trade with the lives of my children in the market square of life, die suddenly, in the name of Jesus.

21. Arrow of affliction fired to stagnate the progress of my children this year, backfire, in the name of Jesus.

22. In this year, Angels of God, locate and pursue the helpers of my children to them and let their situation change, in the name of Jesus.

23. Garment of shame and disgrace prepared by domestic witchcraft for my children to wear, tear to pieces, catch fire and burn to ashes, in the name of Jesus.

24. In this New Year, O Lord feed my children with honey from the rock and give them living water to drink, in the name of Jesus.

25. You God of new beginning open new doors for my children this year and let every door of good thing they knock, open by their own accord, in the name of Jesus.

26. I reject demotion by satanic powers for my children this year. O God of promotion, promote them by fire and give them a glorious beginning, in the name of Jesus.

27. In this year, O Lord, launch my children into great jubilation, celebration and uncommon favours that cannot be explained, in the name of Jesus.

28. As my children enter this year with glorious beginning, they will celebrated and will be celebrated, whether the enemy likes it or not, in the name of Jesus.

29. My Father, let Your fresh fire and anointing of spiritual breakthrough fall upon my children this year, in the name of Jesus.

30. You powers that troubled the destiny of my children last year, go into captivity and let their glory and star rise and shine forth this year, in the name of Jesus.

31. In this year, O Lord, let the divine helpers of my children locate them and let them receive Your surplus mercy, in the name of Jesus.

32. Every door of good things locked against my children last year and fresh doors of opportunities that will move their lives forward this year, hear the word of the Lord, open, in the name of Jesus.

33. O God arise, defend Your interest in the lives of my children and let Your Angels of mercy, favour, blessing and the glory overshadow their lives this year, in the name of Jesus.

34. Holy Spirit, be the Senior Partner, move in the lives of my children this year and let their lives experience spiritual revival in the things of God, in the name of Jesus.

35. Every ancestral power of my father's house monitoring the star of my children last year, you cannot continue this year, Angels of the Living God, smite them with blindness, in the name of Jesus.

36. Shout of congratulations shall bombard the homes of my children this year for remarkable achievement, in the name of Jesus.

37. My Father, do something great, something good, something wonderful in the lives of my children this year that will change the history of their lives, in the name of Jesus.

38. O God arise for the sake of my children this year, disgrace those powers challenging their God and show them that You are their God, in the name of Jesus.

39. Uncommon Favour and Open Heaven Breakthroughs, the lives of my children are available for you, manifest, in the name of Jesus.

40. As the sun appears everyday, O God that changes times and seasons, let the glory of my children that has departed reappear this year and shine in glory, in the name of Jesus.

41. O God, begin afresh in my children and let bad times and evil seasons cease permanently in their lives this year, in the name of Jesus.

42. O God, advertise your greatness in the lives of my children this year and let them be celebrated for signs and wonders, in the name of Jesus.

43. In this year, O Lord, let all inherited limitations to obtaining good things depart from my children and let their season of favour appear by fire, in the name of Jesus.

44. Every good thing my children have been expecting, desiring or pursing in the past year, begin to pursue them, overtake them and possess them in this year, in the name of Jesus.

45. My children shall have no reason to sorrow or be ashamed this year, every power delegated to spoil their joy and happiness, ground open and swallow them, in the name of Jesus.

46. Every seed and root of failure planted in the garden of my children, to hinder their progress in life, I purge you with the blood of Jesus, wither and die, in the name of Jesus.

47. Every satanic contact point in the lives of my children to uproot them from their garden of breakthroughs, be terminated by fire, in the name of Jesus.

48. Every spirit of Kadesh Barnea that kept my children in the wilderness of slavery last year, loose your grip for them to arise and move forward in life this year, in the name of Jesus.

49. Begin to thank God for answered prayers.

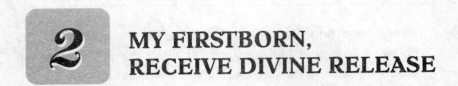

MY FIRSTBORN, RECEIVE DIVINE RELEASE

Praise Worship

Scripture Reading – Numbers 3:40-51

Confession – Genesis 22:17

PRAYER POINTS (Pray with the name of Firstborn)

1. I revoke every satanic decree upon the life, family and prosperity of my first born with the Blood of Jesus, in the name of Jesus.

2. Every satanic roadblock erected to divert the star of my first born and cover his glory, blood of Jesus dismantle them, in the name of Jesus.

3. I raise the staff of prayer to divide the Red Sea standing between my firstborn and his miracle of supernatural promotion, in the name of Jesus.

4. By the Blood of Jesus, I release my first born from the umbrella of any collective captivity, inherited bondage and foundational covenant/curse hindering his/her progress, in the name of Jesus.

5. Rain of affliction, failure and demonic attacks from powers of the father's house, targeted at my firstborn, I stop you by the blood of Jesus, die, in the name of Jesus.

6. Every appointment with sudden and untimely death programmed for my firstborn, I cancel it with the blood of Jesus, in Jesus name.

7. Every power sponsoring repeated problems and resurrection of affliction in the life of my firstborn, to stagnate his/her advancement in life, receive thunder fire of God and die, in the name of Jesus.

8. Every witchcraft padlock used to lockup the marriage, the business, the womb and the brain of my firstborn, Holy Ghost Fire, break them and set them ablaze, in the name of Jesus.

9. Every river of evil family pattern flowing down to my firstborn from my ancestral line, dry up now by fire, in the name of Jesus.

10. Divine power of reformation and restoration fall upon my firstborn and give him/her divine transformation in all areas, in Jesus' name.

11. You my firstborn, I prophesy into your life, God will add value to you, you will always be the head, you will not serve your junior, in Jesus' name.

12. By the power that changes times and season, O God arise, sit on the situation of my firstborn, and let the story of his/her life change for better, in the name of Jesus.

13. O Lord rearrange and reorder the life of my first born for breakthroughs and excellence and let holy transfiguration fall upon him/her, in the name of Jesus.

14. Every stubborn household enemy that has vowed not to forgive but to waste my firstborn, O God, set ambush for him, in Jesus' name.

15. O Lord, do not allow the enemies to celebrate the demotion of my firstborn but promote him/her from ordinary to extraordinary like Jabez, and from zero to hero, in Jesus' name.

16. O Lord, network my first born with divine helpers and catapult him/her from valley of promises to mountain of fulfillment, in Jesus' name.

17. Blood of Jesus, poison and kill the root of every mocking problems in the life of my firstborn and let his problem begin to have problems, in the name of Jesus.

18. Every power detaining my first born in the wilderness of slavery, I strike you with chaos and confusion, release him/her now and die, in the name of Jesus.

19. Every gate of humiliation, wall of sorrow, doors of tragedy, pit of failure and demonic chain of stagnancy assigned against my first born, shatter to pieces by thunder and release your captive, in the name of Jesus.

20. Rain of promotion, rain of supernatural abundance and anointing of breakthroughs, I provoke you by the blood of Jesus, begin to fall on my firstborn, in the name of Jesus.

21. Household wickedness networking with household witchcraft to destroy the colourful destiny of my first born, I judge you by the blood of Jesus, die, in the name of Jesus.

22. I deprogramme and cancel by the blood of Jesus every mandate given to any evil power to supervise and monitor the life of my firstborn, in the name of Jesus.

23. Name of Jesus, blood of Jesus, fire of the Holy Ghost and the armies of heaven, wage war against the stubborn household strongman that says my first born will not make it in life, in the name of Jesus.

ANOINTED DESTINY CHANGING PRAYERS FOR YOUR CHILDREN

24. Oh Lord, let divine earthquake shake down every satanic warehouse harbouring the virtue and potentials of my fist born, in Jesus' name.

25. Every agent of disgrace, backwardness, shame and reproach delegated against my firstborn, ground open and swallow them, in Jesus' name.

26. Every foundational inheritance evil dedication, satanic sacrifice and parental curse, caging my first born from his/her root and magnetizing his/her progress backward, blood of Jesus destroy them, in the name of Jesus.

27. Every good door of progress and prosperity shut by household wickedness against my first born, open now to accelerated advancement, in the name of Jesus.

28. Every spirit of Cain, Esau and Reuben, the life of my firstborn is not for you, therefore die, in the name of Jesus.

29. Angels of the living God, arrest, detain, prosecute and punish all agents of darkness working against the manifestation of divine prophetic agenda for my firstborn, in the name of Jesus.

30. Arrow of insanity, infirmity and paralysis fired into the life of my first, to disgrace his/her life, back fire and go back to your sender, in the name of Jesus.

31. Every satanic embargo blocking, delaying and frustrating the success, the progress and the breakthrough of my first born, expire today, in the name of Jesus.

32. Every stubborn strongman using barriers of limitation against my first born for him/her to die unfulfilled, uncelebrated and unaccomplished, die a shameful death, in the name of Jesus.

33. Blood of Jesus, purge the root of my first born and redeem him/her from every generational and foundational curses and covenant working against his/her moving forward in life, in the name of Jesus.

34. Every spiritual ignorance in my first born that has given the enemy legal right to place embargo of non-achievement upon his/her life, die, in the name of Jesus.

35. Lord Jesus, disconnect my firstborn from all unprofitable relationships and close any door not opened by you, in the name of Jesus.

36. Begin to thank God for answered prayers.

OH LORD, OPEN BOOK OF REMEMBRANCE FOR MY CHILDREN

Praise Worship

Scripture Reading – Esther 6:1-11

Confession: Malachi 3:16

PRAYER POINTS

1. O Lord, open book of remembrance for my children and bombard their lives with expected and unexpected blessings, in the name of Jesus.

2. O Lord, remember my daughters praying for the fruit of the womb and make them pregnant to become mothers of their own children this year like Rachael, in Jesus' name. (Gen. 30:22-23)

3. My Father, remember my children this year and make them plenteous, for good in the name of Jesus (Deut. 28:11)

4. Lord Jesus, open book of remembrance for my children and let the set time to show them Your mercy and favour manifest now, in the name of Jesus. (Ps. 102:13)

5. My Father and my God, open Your book of remembrance for my children, remember them for good and test them with mirth, in the name of Jesus. (Neh. 13:31b)

6. My Father, let Your mercy open book of remembrance for my children look for job to meet divine helpers and get job that will make them happy and comfortable in life, in Jesus' name.

7. O Lord, remember my children who are still unmarried, magnetize them to their rightful partners and promote them from singles to married this year, in the name of Jesus.

8. Father Lord, remember my children seeking placement in higher institution, let mercy speak for them and give the desire of their heart, in the name of Jesus.

9. O Lord, my Father, let book of remembrance for repositioning, promotion and elevation be opened for my children this year, in the name of Jesus.

10. Goliath of frustration, manipulating the celebration of my children's day of honour, glory and jubilation, I cut off your head, die, in the name of Jesus.

11. O Lord my Father, let there be a divine rearrangement in the power house of my children's school and working place that will bring them from obscurity to limelight, in the name of Jesus.

12. O Lord, let the enemies of my children make mistake that will cause the book of remembrance to be opened for their elevation, in the name of Jesus.

13. As the Lord liveth, book of remembrance that will change the story of my children, give them new name and make their case a miracle and testimony, open by fire, in the name of Jesus.

14. Every satanic influence organized to cage, to torment and waste the labour of my children, scatter, in the name of Jesus.

15. Every satanic agent of mocking, shame and disgrace programmed and promoted to torment my children in the land of the living, die a shameful death, in the name of Jesus.

16. I release the spirit and fire of confusion, disaffection and

undiluted hatred into the camp of the enemies preventing the book of remembrance to open for my children, in the name of Jesus.

17. Holy Ghost arise, with thunder and lighting to arrest, prosecute and execute judgment of death upon all stubborn pursuers, pursuing my children out of their place of honour, in the name of Jesus.

18. Sword of judgement and vengeance of God, pursue, attack and destroy every evil power attacking the staff of bread of my children, in the name of Jesus.

19. After the order of Haman, the enemy that wants my children to die shall be the one to put garment of honour upon them, cover their head with crown of glory and put in their hand, staff of authority, in Jesus' name

20. Lord Jesus, let the book of remembrance of the good deeds of my children speak for them and usher them into their next level, in the name of Jesus.

21. Every satanic old prophet, assigned to mislead my children and hinder their fulfillment in life, die, suddenly, in the name of Jesus.

22. The book of remembrance that will make my children to be celebrated and to jubilate, that the enemy has closed, open now by fire, in the name of Jesus.

23. O Lord, remember my children for special honour that will distinguish them like Daniel, Joseph and Elizabeth, in the name of Jesus.

24. _____ receive the key of heaven to open all the doors of goodness that the enemy has closed against you, in the name of Jesus.

25. The book of remembrance that You have opened for my children, O Lord, do not allow the enemy to close it, in the name of Jesus.

26. You the book of remembrance of my children hear the word of the Lord, open now by fire and increase them more and more in all areas of their lives, in the name of Jesus.

27. O Lord, open book of remembrance for my children and let helpers connected with their destiny, remember them and favour them, in the name of Jesus.

28. Begin to thank God for answered prayers.

4. O LORD, LAUNCH MY CHILDREN INTO SEASONS OF NEW THINGS

Praise Worship

Bible Reading:- Isaiah 41:17 – 20

Confession: Isaiah 43:18-19

PRAYER POINTS

1. By Your power that knows no impossibility, O Lord, launch my children into their season of new things, in the name of Jesus.

2. O God that changes times and seasons, let my children begin to experience seasons of new things in their lives, in the name of Jesus.

3. O God of wonders, do what will be described as a Miracle beyond arguments by those who have been looking down on my children, in the name of Jesus.

4. For the reason of my children being in their season of new things, as they are getting married, they will be naming their children and dedicating their new house in the name of Jesus.

5. Lord Jesus, heal every unpleasant water around the lives of my children so that their breakdown will become breakthroughs, their burden will become blessings and their groaning shall turn to glory, in the name of Jesus.

6. Thou creative power of God, perform creative miracles in the womb of my children to produce their set of twins this year, in the name of Jesus.

7. God of promotion, promote my children from single to married, from tenant to landlord and from employee to employer of labour, as they enter into their season of new things, in the name of Jesus.

8. Father Lord, as my children enter into their season of great things, build the necessary structure and take them to their next level, in the name of Jesus.

9. By fire by favour, O Lord, let the story of my children change, give them a new name, put a new song in their mouth, make them a positive wonder and let them be celebrated, in the name of Jesus.

10. By the power that divided the Red Sea, O Lord, separate my children from failure, hardship, poverty, lack, sickness, and push them into their seasons of new things, in the name of Jesus.

11. Every evil chain of slavery preventing my children from moving into their seasons of new things, break to pieces and burn to ashes, in the name of Jesus.

12. Every ancestral, inherited and collective embargo, placed in the way of my children, to hinder them moving into their seasons of new things, be revoked by fire, in the name of Jesus.

13. Every power of limitation, anointing of stagnation and demoting spirit, on evil assignment to truncate the journey of my children into their season of new things, be swept away by the broom of destruction, in the name of Jesus.

14. Every stubborn strongman, household wickedness and household witchcraft, from both sides of the family line of my children, networking to frustrate their seasons of new things, I set you against yourselves, fight and destroy yourselves, in Jesus' name.

15. Every covenant of sudden and untimely death with this year, programmed by powers of darkness, to harvest the lives of my children and prevent their seasons of new things, break by the blood of Jesus and backfire, in the name of Jesus.

16. Emptiers, wasters and devourers of the father/mothers house, assigned to waste the harvest of my children in their seasons of new things, your assignment is over, die, in the name of Jesus.

17. O Lord, redeem the past of my children, soak their present in Your blood and secure their future with divine insurance, so that they can accomplish their season of new thing, in the name of Jesus.

18. Every witchcraft trader advertising the lives of my children for sale, in order to harvest their lives and terminate their entry into the seasons of new things, what do you think you are doing, die in the name of Jesus.

19. Every family idol, family tree, witchcraft coven, evil altar, holding the destiny of my children in bondage, so as not to into seasons of new things, thunder fire of God, set them ablaze, in the name of Jesus.

20. Sing this song 7 (seven) times as you lift up the photograph of your children.

    Do something new in their lives, something new in their lives

    Do something new in their lives today,

    O God that answereth by fire, You will answer them by fire,

    You will answer them by fire, today.

21. Begin to thank God for answered prayers.

5 OH LORD, DELIVER MY CHILDREN

Praise Worship

Bible Reading – Dan. 3:16-30

Confession: Daniel 6:27

PRAYER POINTS

1. O Lord, deliver my children from the binding effects of collective and inherited curses and covenants placed upon both sides of their ancestral line, in the name of Jesus.

2. O Lord, give my children divine insurance and deliver them from accidents, tragedy, kidnaping for rituals, armed robbery and fire disaster, in the name of Jesus.

3. As You delivered David from the mouth of the Lions, O Lord, deliver my children from being devoured by earthly Lions, in the name of Jesus.

4. As You saved Sheddrach, Masharc and Abednego from the furnace of fire, fourth man in the furnace, deliver my children from the fire of the enemy, in the name of Jesus.

5. As You delivered Israel, Your people, from bondage in Egypt, Father Lord, deliver my children from the ancestral powers holding their lives in bondage, in the name of Jesus.

6. As You delivered Mardeccai from untimely death planned by Haman, O Lord, deliver my children from sudden, untimely death and let their enemy die in their place, in the name of Jesus.

7. As You delivered Joseph from the envious conspiracy of household wickedness to abort his destiny, O Lord, deliver my children to fulfill their divine destiny, in the name of Jesus.

8. As You delivered David from 21 attempts by King Saul to kill him, O Lord, deliver my children from all the secret plans of their enemies to terminate their lives, in the name of Jesus.

9. As Haman was made to announce the glory of Mordecai and Balaam to bless the Israelites, o Lord, let the Haman of my children announce their glory and their Balaam to bless them, in the name of Jesus.

10. As You disgraced King Nebuchadnezzar for asking of the God of the Hebrew captives that can deliver them, O Lord, deliver my children and make their enemies know that You are their God, in the name of Jesus.

11. As You silenced the boasting of King Senacherib and made him to die by the sword of his own children, O Lord, deliver my children from the wicked powers terrorizing them and make them die a shameful death, in the name of Jesus.

12. As You made Pharaoh to pursue Israel to the Red and perished there, O Lord let all the evil pursuers of my children, perish in their own Red Sea, in the name of Jesus.

13. As You delivered Peter miraculously from the prison, O Lord deliver my children from the prison house of the enemy with a miracle of "how did it happen" in the name of Jesus.

ANOINTED DESTINY CHANGING PRAYERS FOR YOUR CHILDREN

14. As You disgraced Goliath and delivered Israel from his oppression and suppression, O Lord, deliver my children from the oppression and suppression of the powers of their father's house, in the name of Jesus.

15. O Lord, deliver my children from every satanic embargo placed upon their marital, financial, business, project, academic and spiritual breakthroughs, in the name of Jesus.

16. From now to the end of this year, Angels of Jehovah God, establish the going out and coming in of my children so that Satan will not use them to balance his account, in the name of Jesus.

17. O Lord my Father deliver my children from the power of sin, Satan and the flesh and give them daily victory by the blood of Jesus, in the name of Jesus.

18. Lord Jesus, deliver my children from the bondage of evil thought, thought of evil and evil imaginations, create in them a new heart and renew a right spirit within them, in the name of Jesus.

19. O Lord God, deliver my children from the works of the flesh and lusts of the flesh that can hinder their heaven, in the name of Jesus.

20. Lord Jesus, deliver my children from the lies of the devil and uphold them with Your Spirit of righteousness, in the name of Jesus.

21. O Lord, deliver the soul of my children from destruction, their eyes from tears and their feet from stumbling physically or spiritually, in the name of Jesus.

22. From the battle of holy people and known people, O Lord, deliver my children, in the name of Jesus.

23. From the punishment of the sins of the ancestors to which my children are not party to, but is now affecting them, O Lord deliver them, in the name of Jesus.

24. O Lord, deliver my children from the wicked devices of secret enemies, household enemies and unfriendly friends planning perpetual battles against them, in the name of Jesus.

25. Sing this Song:

    Deliver them, deliver them, deliver my children

    By Your fire, by Your power

    Deliver them O Lord.

26. Begin to praise God for answer prayers.

6 IT'S TIME FOR MY CHILDREN TO RISE AND SHINE

Praise Worship

Scripture Reading – Isaiah 60:1-6

Confession – Sing this song 3 times

"my children shall rise and shine (2ce)
Lord Jehovah is able to do all things
My children shall rise and shine

PRAYER POINTS

1. Every pot of darkness caging the star of my children from rising and shining, break by fire, in the name of Jesus.

2. Any power of the father's house, that needs to die for God to move my children forward and begin to shine in glory, what are you waiting for, die now in the name of Jesus.

3. Every environmental embargo preventing the star of my children from rising and shining, break now by fire, in the name of Jesus.

4. Every problem in the background of my children, that has root in their foundation, receive total deliverance and divine solution, in the name of Jesus.

5. O Lord my father, defend, deliver and preserve the star of my children from the attack of household wickedness and household witchcraft caging them from rising and shining in the name of Jesus (Read Isaiah 31:5)

6. O Lord, arise revive your grace, your mercy and your favour upon my children and let their star arise and shine in the name of Jesus.

7. Every power consulting idol against the stars of my children, I command the idol to slap you and swallow you in the name of Jesus.

8. O Lord, by your creative power, touch every area of my children's lives and give them the desired change now in the name of Jesus.

9. Every soul hunter, shooting arrows of wickedness and destruction at the star and destiny of my children, your time is up, die in the name of Jesus.

10. Every strongman of the father's house sitting on the beneficial potentials of my children in order to hold their star captive, enter into captivity and die in the name of Jesus (Read Rev. 13:10)

11. Every problem in the lives of my children that rises with the sun and the moon and clouding their star, die in the name of Jesus.

12. Thou star of my children, arise, shine and refuse to set at noon day in the name of Jesus.

13. I draw a line with the blood of Jesus, between my children and the powers of the father's house, saying "No Way" for them to rise and shine this year, in the name of Jesus.

14. Every good blessing I missed in my life shall not by-pass my children in the name of Jesus.

15. Any power that wants to turn my children's morning to night, die in the name of Jesus.

16. My father, let every architect of failure and stagnancy for my children be disgraced and convert them to outstanding achievers in Jesus' name.

17. Lord Jesus, let every anti-progress altar, fashioned against my children, be dismantled by thunder fire and enlarge their coasts beyond their widest imagination, in the name of Jesus.

18. By the power that moved Moses forward at the Red Sea, O Lord, move my children forward by your hand of fire and catapult them to greatness like Daniel, in the name of Jesus.

19. Anointing to rise and shine and become the most prominent among their family line, fall upon my children, in the name of Jesus.

20. The glory of my children that has departed, reappear now because it is time for my children to rise and shine, in the name of Jesus.

21. I claim explosive miracle of "come and see" and "how did it happen" for my children in every department of their lives, in the name of Jesus.\

22. Every power, standing at the gates of my children greatness tying them down and suppressing their elevation to rise and shine, your time is up, die in the name of Jesus.

23. Every witchcraft Pharaoh, saying my children will not rise and shine, and reach their promised land this year, you are a liar, die in your own Red Sea, in the name of Jesus.

24. Lord Jesus, let an everlasting reproach, a perpetual shame and double destruction fall upon the wicked star killers, assigned against my children, in the name of Jesus.

25. Every foundation and pillar of witchcraft in my family line, working against the moving forward of my children to rise and shine, be destroyed by the blood of Jesus.

26. Every evil vision and prophecy by false prophets, that my children have accepted before, that is taking good things from them, be neutralized by the blood of Jesus.

27. Every deposit of witchcraft power and hidden covenants polluting the lives of my children, break by the blood of Jesus and go back to your sender, in the name of Jesus.

28. All the virtues of my children that have been washed away in any body of water, I recall you by the blood of Jesus, locate them now, in the name of Jesus.

29. Every negative writing in the circle of the moon, that is manifesting against my children, month by month, be blotted out by the blood of Jesus and attack your owner, in the name of Jesus.

30. Every wicked law and evil word programmed in the star of my children, to generate seasonal failure and stagnation, you shall not be established, die, in the name of Jesus.

31. Sing this song 3 times as you wave their photographs to heaven.

    My children shall be blessed
    Their stars will sure shine   } 2ce
    And I shall rejoice over them

32. Begin to thank God for answered prayers.

7 MY CHILDREN MUST PROSPER

Praise Worship

Bible Reading: Deut. 28:11-12

Confession III John 2

PRAYER POINTS

1. Where is the Lord God of Abraham, Isaac and Jacob, arise and revive the divine potentials of my children for prosperity, in the name of Jesus.

2. O Lord my God, create profitable opportunities for my children that will push them into their garden of prosperity, in the name of Jesus.

3. Anointing for all round prosperity fall upon my children and break every yoke of poverty in their lives, in the name of Jesus.

4. Father Lord, let Your rain of prosperity fall upon my children that will provoke unexplainable testimony in their lives, in the name of Jesus.

5. This year, whether the devil likes it or not my children will experience bombardment of prosperity in all areas of their lives, in the name of Jesus.

6. Every power holding the prosperity of my children captive, enough is enough release it and die, in the name of Jesus.

7. Every stronghold of poverty created against prosperity in the lives of my children, I pull you down by fire, in the name of Jesus.

8. Every silent bondage in the lives of my children closing doors of prosperity against them break by fire and burn to ashes, in the name of Jesus.

9. O God of performance, perform wonders in the lives of my children that will make them prosper, in the name of Jesus.

10. O God of possibility, decree divine possibilities to every area in the lives of my children that will make their prosperity possible, in the name of Jesus.

11. You the cloud of poverty over the lives of my children clear away and be converted to rain of prosperity, in the name of Jesus.

12. Every anti-breakthrough and anti-prosperity forces assigned against my children, blood of Jesus destroy them, Holy Ghost fire set them ablaze, in the name of Jesus.

13. Lord Jesus, deliver into the hands of my children the keys of the hidden treasures of this land that will promote their prosperity, in the name of Jesus.

14. You the spirit of ... (pick from the under-listed) working against the prosperity in the lives of my children, I challenge you with the blood of Jesus, die, in the name of Jesus.

    (a) Borrowing (b) Labouring in vain (c) Anti-success

    (d) Satanic enchantment (e) Bad luck (f) Lack of good relationship (g) Slavery (h) Leaking and bewitched pockets (i) Ignorance (j) Non-achievement (k) Financial stagnation (l) Fake comfort (m) Anti-breakthrough (n) Non-challant attitude (o) Insufficiency

15. Every strength and power of environmental altar and satanic priests, ministering in any evil altar against the prosperity of my children, die by fire in the name of Jesus.

16. Every seed of inherited, collective and acquired poverty working against divine prosperity in the lives of my children, I bind and I cast you out, catch fire and burn to ashes, in the name of Jesus.

17. Every curse of poverty placed upon my family line, now working against prosperity of my children, blood of Jesus break them and deliver my children, in the name of Jesus.

18. Every witchcraft covenant of poverty made by the living or the dead in the father/mother house of my children, break by fire, back fire, in the name of Jesus.

19. Every sponsored dream of poverty, by wicked and stubborn household witchcraft, clear away by the Name of Jesus, Blood of Jesus and Fire of the Holy Ghost, in the name of Jesus.

20. Every cage of poverty holding the prosperity of my children in bondage, roast to ashes and every evil bank established against their prosperity, be liquidated by fire, in the name of Jesus.

21. O God arise, give my children the grace that will terminate disgrace and prosperity that will completely bury poverty in their lives, in the name of Jesus.

22. Sing this song:

    In the name of Jesus, my children, my children, my children

    In the name of Jesus, my children, must prosper.

23. Begin to thank God for answered prayers.

8 OH LORD, BLESS MY CHILDREN

Praise Worship

Scripture Reading – Deut 28:1-13

Confession: Gen. 12:2-3

PRAYER POINTS

1. O Lord, water the garden of my children with divine blessings and make them a watered garden where blessings will never cease, in the name of Jesus.

2. In the going and coming of my children, O Lord, let people go out of their way to bless them, in the name of Jesus.

3. The blessing that no one has ever received in the family line of my children, O Lord, let it be the portion of my children, in the name of Jesus.

4. My Father, lead my children to the source of their blessings, bless them with the blessings of heaven and make them channels of blessing to their generation, in the name of Jesus.

5. Oh Lord, according to your promise to Father Abraham, bless those who bless my children and curse those who curse them, in the name of Jesus.

6. Father Lord, let the wind of fire blow against all powers sitting on the blessings due to my children, unseat them and release their blessings, in the name of Jesus.

7. O Lord, let the east wind pull down every stronghold of wickedness in the environment of my children, militating against their blessings, in the name of Jesus.

8. Every power that is making blessings of Abraham to appear, disappear and pass over my children, your time is up, die, in the name of Jesus.

9. O Lord, order the steps of my children to coincide with unexpected blessings and let blessing meet blessing in their lives in the name of Jesus.

10. Every satanic cage, prison or warehouse holding the blessings of God for my children captive, receive thunder fire, catch fire and release their blessings, in the name of Jesus.

11. Every rock spirit, forest spirit, water spirit and ancestral tree holding the blessings of my children in bondage release their blessings and die, in the name of Jesus.

12. Satan will not use any of my children to balance his account this year in order to abort their blessings; in the name of Jesus.

13. Every satanic cobweb and bewitchment programmed against divine blessings for my children, catch fire and die, in the name of Jesus.

14. Every satanic masquerade in the dream pursuing my children in order to steal their blessings, pursue yourself to destruction, in the name of Jesus.

15. My Father, Your word says "in blessing I will bless you, in multiplying I will multiply you", any power contending with my children for their blessings, heavens, contend with them, in the name of Jesus.

16. Oh Lord my Father, let all the blessings of the Bible, pursue, overtake and settle with my children, in the name of Jesus.

17. Lord Jesus, bless the womb of my daughter-in-laws for instant pregnancy that will remove reproach and mockery of barrenness from their lives, in the name of Jesus.

18. O Lord, bless the labour of the hands of my children, to prevent unprofitable hardwork, as working like elephant and eating like ant, in the name of Jesus.

19. Every day as my children go out, let them meet that man/woman that will help them and bless them, in the name of Jesus.

20. O Lord, pronounce blessings of promotion upon my children that are working and move them to their next level, in Jesus' name.

21. Lord Jesus, let blessing join mercy and favour to produce outstanding breakthroughs (financial, marital, business, academic etc) in the lives of my children, in the name of Jesus.

22. O Lord, let every satanic rituals and demonic sacrifices before ancestral shrines, directed against blessings, mercy and favour for my children, back fire, in the name of Jesus.

23. Blessings of God and blessing from God, the lives of my children are waiting for you, wherever you are, appear, in the name of Jesus.

24. Every wicked power attacking the blessings of my children, so that they may live in shame and die in shame, you are a liar, sleep the sleep of death, in the name of Jesus.

25. All the blessings of my children that the stubborn strongman of the father's house has cursed, I reverse the curse by the blood of Jesus, carry your evil load and die, in the name of Jesus.

26. Every hold of sin in the lives of my children that will close heaven of blessing against them, catch fire and burn to ashes, in the name of Jesus.

27. O God of Elijah, arise in Your power, take my children from the crowd and give them special blessing sin the business that will put joy in their heart and laughter in their mouth, in Jesus' name.

28. O God of Elijah, arise in Your power, take my children from the crowd and give them special blessings in their business that will put joy in their heart and laughter in their mouth, in Jesus' name.

29. O God of Israel, arise in Your power, take my children from the crowd and give them special blessings in their academic that will promote them to shining stars and high fliers, in Jesus' name.

30. You my children, I pronounce the priestly blessing in Num. 6:24-26 upon you.

    "The Lord bless you and keep you. The Lord make His face shine upon you and be gracious unto you. The Lord lift up His countenance upon you and give you peace."

31. Sing this song 7 times as you wave their photographs:

    "Abraham blessings are yours, all my children

    Abraham blessings are yours,

    You are blessed in the morning,

    In the noon, in the night

    Abraham blessings are yours.

32. Begin to thank God for answered prayers.

9 OH LORD, REMEMBER MY CHILDREN FOR GOOD

Praise Worship

Bible Reading: - I Sam. 1:9-19

Confession: Neh. 13:31b

PRAYER POINTS

1. O Lord my Father, remember my children with your mercy and favour and raise divine helpers for them, in the name of Jesus.

2. By the power that divided the Red Sea, O Lord remember my children that are looking for job for good, open a way of good job for them that will make their case a miracle and a testimony this year, in the name of Jesus.

3. O Lord that remembered Hannah, Sarah and Elizabeth, remember my children that believe You for the fruit of the womb for good and make them proud mothers of their own children this year, in the name of Jesus.

4. O God that gave Rebecca to Isaac by divine intervention, remember my children that are praying for divine partner and magnetise them to their rightful partner this year, in the name of Jesus.

5. My children that are seeking for admission, O Lord remember them for good, raise divine helpers that will help them secure suitable admission, in the name of Jesus.

6. The Promotion of my children that has been delayed and denied, O God arise and cause the promotion to be released by fire, in the name of Jesus.

7. The marriage of my children that is at the verge of collapse, Jesus the Prince of Peace, arise and restore the relationship with Your resurrection power, in the name of Jesus.

8. O Lord, remember my children with Your mercy and favour and bless them on all sides, in the name of Jesus.

9. O Lord, remember my children for good, let their story change to the best and give them a new song this year, in the name of Jesus.

10. O Lord, remember my children for good and break every satanic embargo on their way of progress, in the name of Jesus.

11. Any power from the Fathers/mothers house arresting good things in the lives of my children, who ever you are, release them and die, in the name of Jesus.

12. O Lord, remember my children and rewrite their story, in the name of Jesus.

13. Wherever my children are expecting and where they are not, let mercy speak for them and let people compete to help and bless them, in the name of Jesus.

14. O Lord, remember my children for good and let all the closed doors to their breakthroughs open by fire, in the name of Jesus.

15. O Lord, remember my children for good and let all dry bones in any area of their lives come alive, in the name of Jesus.

16. O Lord, remember my children for good, do the uncommon and unusual to make them sing their song and dance their dance this year, in the name of Jesus.

17. O Lord remember my children for good, do that which the enemy thinks is impossible in the lives with Your power of possibility, in the name of Jesus.

18. O Lord remember my children for good and let all inherited, collective, ancestral curses and covenants working against them break forever, in the name of Jesus.

19. Say this 21 times – O Lord remember my children for good this year, in the name of Jesus.

20. Sing this song 7 times.

    Remember my children (2ce)

    Remember my children, O Lord

    Remember my children (2ce)

    Remember my children, O Lord.

10 MY CHILDREN SHALL RECEIVE DIVINE VISITATION

Praise Worship

Bible Reading – 2 Peter 2:9-12

Confession: Psalm 106:4-5

PRAYER POINTS

1. Divine Angels of my children, visit them and take up your respective assignments in their lives, in the name of Jesus.

2. Angel of death, refuse to visit my children because they will fulfill the number of their days in the land of the living, in the name of Jesus.

3. Lord Jesus, let my children receive Angelic visitation like Zechariah for a turn around breakthrough that will disgrace in their lives, in the name of Jesus.

4. O Lord, let my children receive divine visitation like Hannah, Sarah and Elizabeth and let their season of fruitfulness begin now, in the name of Jesus.

5. My Father, visit my children in the land of their affliction, turn their mourning to dancing, put laughter in their mouth, joy in their heart and remove their reproach, in the name of Jesus.

6. O Lord my God, visit every dry region in the lives of my children with early and later rain that will produce harvest of good things for them, in the name of Jesus.

7. Lord Jesus, deliver my children from all powers oppressing, suppressing and intimidating their lives and visit the camp of the enemy with Your fury and snares, in the name of Jesus.

8. After the order of Rom. 8:19, O Lord, visit my children with the power to manifest, excel and become advertisement of Your power, as they move higher like eagle, in the name of Jesus.

9. God of Heaven, let the heavens of my children open for divine visitation that will make people to celebrate and jubilate with them, in the name of Jesus.

10. After the order of the man at the Pool of Bethesaida, O Lord give my children special visitation that will disgrace every longstanding problems in their lives, in the name of Jesus.

11. My father, give my children visitation of supernatural surprises and do the unbelievable and the humanly impossible to advertise Your glory, in the name of Jesus.

12. After the order of Apostle Peter, (Acts 12:4-16) let my children receive Angelic visitation that will set them free from every satanic prisons holding them in bondage, in the name of Jesus.

13. O God that changes times and seasons, let my children receive visitation of divine restoration and turn again of their captivity, in the name of Jesus.

14. In this year, Lord Jesus, give my children divine visitation that will take them out of the crowd in the family line, in the name of Jesus.

15. My Father, the lives of my children are available for you, wherever they are, let them experience Your divine visitation, in the name of Jesus.

16. As You turned the situation of Jabez around, O Lord give my children divine visitation that will remove barrier of darkness and release their key of breakthrough, in the name of Jesus.

17. Every wicked power of the Father's house that is behind the sufferings of my children, Angels of the living God, feed them with bread of adversity and water of affliction, in the name of Jesus.

18. Every witchcraft burial of good things in the lives of my children, be liberated by the resurrection power in the blood of Jesus and come alive, in the name of Jesus.

19. Every power of the father's house standing on the way of divine visitation for my children this year, die, in the name of Jesus.

20. By Your divine visitation, O Lord, revive Your grace, Your mercy and Your favour in the lives of my children, that will make their case uncommon story in this generation, in the name of Jesus.

21. Every personality ordained to help and bless my children, wherever you are "APPEAR" and locate them, in the name of Jesus.

22. Every evil foundational tree of the father's house preventing divine visitation in the lives of my children, be uprooted to the root by thunder and burn to ashes, in the name of Jesus.

23. The Joseph of my children will not die in the pit, die in the prison or die in Portiphas house, but receive divine visitation that will promote them to their place of honour, in the name of Jesus.

24. Any ancestral power frustrating any area of my children's lives in order to discourage them from receiving divine visitation, receive multiple destruction, in the name of Jesus.

25. Every ancestral embargo, inherited bondage and chain of slavery binding my children from moving into the realm of divine visitation, die, in the name of Jesus.

26. As Ruth the Moabites receive divine visitation and become the grandmother of our Lord Jesus Christ, O Lord visit my children, no matter their background and use them for Your glory, in the name of Jesus.

27. As the captain of the host of the Lord visited Joshua during the battle of Jericho to fight for them, O Lord arise and fight all the battles of my children for them, in the name of Jesus.

28. Begin to praise the Lord for answered prayers.

11 HEAVEN OF MY CHILDREN, OPEN

Praise Worship

Scripture Reading – Isaiah 60:9-22

Confession – Isaiah 64:1

PRAYER POINTS

1. Lord, let the heaven of my children open and anoint them for favour this year in the name of Jesus.
2. I separate evil from the portion of my children and cast stagnancy out of their seat of progress in the name of Jesus.
3. As the heaven of my children open this year, they shall not be joint-heirs with failure and stagnancy in the name of Jesus.
4. O Lord, command the heaven of my children to open and let your altar of mercy speak on their behalf this year, in the name of Jesus.
5. Every grip of satan over the heaven of my children, loose your hold and let the story of their lives change to the best, in the name of Jesus.
6. Every power that does not want my children to experience open heavens of accelerated breakthroughs this year, your time is up, die, in the name of Jesus.
7. Every cloud of darkness covering the open heavens of my children, clear away by fire, in the name of Jesus.

8. I receive open heavens for my children this year and I command the heavens to cease to carry warfare into their lives in the name of Jesus.

9. Every inherited spiritual handicap, causing disgrace in the lives of my children, loose your hold and die, in the name of Jesus.

10. Every evil wind blowing against the lives, business, finances marriage and health of my children, here the commandment of Christ, 'Peace be still' in the name of Jesus.

11. You the heaven of my children that has turned to brass, and making the blessing of God to pass over them, open now by fire and by thunder in the name of Jesus.

12. Every power of the father's house, trying to naked and put my children to open shame, receive Angelic whip, fall down and die, in the name of Jesus.

13. Every Satanic driver, operating Satanic diversion, to drive my children to the wrong road of life, receive arrow of destruction and die, in the name of Jesus.

14. As the heavens of my children open this year, O Lord, order their steps to coincide with favour, mercy and blessing, in the name of Jesus.

15. O Lord, do not allow my children to pay the debt they did not owe or reap satanic harvest of their parents; in the name of Jesus.

16. Open heavens, change the portion of my children and let them have a life changing experience this year, in the name of Jesus.

17. Lord Jesus, let the heavens of my children open this year and do the impossible, the unusual and the unexpected in their lives in the name of Jesus.

18. I set the blood of Jesus between satan and the open heavens of my children and I command them to enter into new era of progress in the name of Jesus.

19. Every fetish material dropped on the ground to attack and subdue my children, be rendered impotent, go back and attack your owner, in the name of Jesus.

20. Every conscious and unconscious covenant working against the open heavens of my children, break now by the blood of Jesus, in the name of Jesus.

21. Every curse of stagnancy preventing my children from entering into their open heavens, be nullified by the blood of Jesus, in the name of Jesus.

22. Every satanic certificate of ownership and occupancy in the open heavens of my children, be revoked by the blood of Jesus, in the name of Jesus.

23. Every satanic agent summoning my children to the dust, and using the dust to do them evil, I turn the dust against you, die, in the name of Jesus.

24. Anything in my family line, blocking the heavens of my children from the perfect will of God, clear away by fire, in the name of Jesus.

25. O Lord, put Your salt into the source of my children and uproot anything in their root that is affecting their open heavens, in the name of Jesus.

26. Any power of the father's house that says my children will not enjoy open heavens this year, you are a liar, angels of the living God smite them with blindness, in the name of Jesus.

27. Every stubborn Goliath, occupying the garden of my children and their open heavens, receive stone of fire, fall down and die, in the name of Jesus.

28. You my children, I prophecy into your lives, receive divine visitation, enter into seasons of harvest and enjoy covenant of peace this year, in the name of Jesus.

29. O Lord my God, as you have prepared open heavens for my children, prepare them also for heaven, in the name of Jesus.

30. Begin to thank God for answered prayers.

OH LORD, FIGHT FOR MY CHILDREN

Praise Worship

Bible Reading: Deut. 20:1-4

Confession: III Chro. 20:15

PRAYER POINTS

1. O God arise, use all the weapons in Your armoury to fight and destroy the wicked and stubborn enemies of my children, in the name of Jesus.

2. O God my Father, let the words of the Scripture in Psalm 35:1-8 work against all the combined enemies of my children from both sides of their family, in the name of Jesus.

3. Lion of the Tribe of Judah, fight for my children as You did for Daniel and let their enemies become easy prey in the den of lion prepared for my children, in the name of Jesus.

4. O God that answereth by fire, arise in Your power, fight for my children as You did for three Hebrew boys and let their enemies be roasted in their own furnace of fire, in the name of Jesus.

5. Anywhere the enemies of my children carry their matter to, to do them evil either to witchcraft coven, evil altar, occult centre, marine kingdom or forest demons, blood of Jesus, fight for my children in the name of Jesus.

6. Every masquerade of household witchcraft, attacking my children in their sleep, in order to terminate their destiny, die by thunder, in the name of Jesus.

7. Every enemy of my children, defiling their God, be put to open shame and double disgrace, after the order of Senecarib, in the name of Jesus.

8. O Lord, raise a David to fight and cut off the head of every Goliath and strongman from both sides of my children's family line, in the name of Jesus.

9. Name of Jesus, Blood of Jesus, Fire of the Holy Ghost, fight all the battles of my children for them and avenge them of their adversaries, in the name of Jesus.

10. My Father and my God, fight for my children and let the wickedness of the wicked of their father's house cease over their lives, in the name of Jesus.

11. O Lord fight for my children and let their stubborn enemies enter into the trap set for my children and be buried in the grave dug for them, in the name of Jesus.

12. Lord God, by Your Supernatural power, fight for my children and let every Ahitophel giving evil counsel against them commit suicide by hanging, in the name of Jesus.

13. My Father, expose every enemy engaging my children in secret battle, frustrate their tokens and let their evil plans backfire, in the name of Jesus.

14. Lord Jesus, fight for my children and let their wicked enemies that came upon them from within and without sleep the sleep of death, in the name of Jesus.

15. I place my children under the cross of Christ, cover them with the blood of Jesus and shield them with wall of fire against every wicked attack of their enemies, in the name of Jesus.

16. Lord Jesus send terrifying noises into the camp of the enemies of my children, confuse their language and let them begin to fight and destroy themselves, in the name of Jesus.

17. Father Lord, empower my children to pursue, overtake and recover every good thing spiritual robbers and envious enemies have stolen from them seven fold, in the name of Jesus.

18. O Lord, let the Sun, the Moon and the Stars in their curses fight from heaven for my children, against the enemies attacking their peace, progress and prosperity, in the name of Jesus.

19. Heaven, arise, fight against all the invisible and unknown enemies attacking the work, business and marriage of my children, in the name of Jesus.

20. Sing this song 7 (seven) times as you wave their photographs.

    (Fun awon Omo) Ina Olorun, AraOlorun, manamonaOlorun

    Bere sin i ja fun nwon O, ja fun nwon, ajasegun

21. Begin to thank God for answered prayers.

13 SATAN WILL NOT HARVEST MY CHILDREN

Praise Worship

Scripture Reading – Jeremiah 5:17-26

Confession – Isaiah 44:25

PRAYER POINTS

1. The ministry of Satan to kill, to steal and to destroy will not prosper in the lives of my children, in the name of Jesus.

2. Every hidden altar of my father's house affecting the destiny of my children, catch fire and burn to ashes, in the name of Jesus.

3. Every gathering of satanic agents calling the name of my children for errand in the spirit world, tempest of God, destroy them now, in the name of Jesus.

4. Every satanic gang-up and evil supervision to demote the progress of my children, scatter by thunder, in the name of Jesus.

5. I declare that children will not be used for satanic experiment and be wasted but they will live a honourable and dignified life, in the name of Jesus.

6. I declare that my children will celebrate Jesus and they shall be celebrated, any power waiting to celebrate the failure of my children shall die, in the name of Jesus.

7. I prophesy that he sun of my children shall not set in the noon day, any power that wants me to weep over my children, shall receive baptism of sorrow, in the name of Jesus.

8. Every witchcraft verdict designed to harvest the God-given potentials of my children; I command your plans to backfire, in Jesus' name.

9. Every evil altar and satanic priest raised to harvest good things in the lives of my children, you are wasting your time, catch fire and die, in the name of Jesus.

10. I prophesy into the lives of my children that none of them shall be wasted or harvested by evil powers of the father's house, but shall flourish like a palm tree, in the name of Jesus.

11. Every stubborn strongman delegated to enforce hereditary handicap in order to downgrade and harvest the lives of my children, somersault and die, in the name of Jesus.

12. Every power that acquired witchcraft spirit and familiar spirit because of any of my children, use your power to destroy yourself, in the name of Jesus.

13. Every inherited wicked plantation in the lives of my children, be uprooted to the root, in the name of Jesus.

14. Every instrument of bewitchment affecting the breakthroughs of any of my children, be rendered impotent now, in the name of Jesus.

15. Every point of contact of the devil in the lives of my children, I terminate you by fire, in the name of Jesus.

16. O Lord, confound the language of stubborn household witchcraft and household wickedness networking to harvest the lives of my children, in the name of Jesus.

17. Every ancestral witchcraft tree in my family house harbouring the blessings of my children, receive the thunder of God, release their blessings and die, in the name of Jesus.

18. God of Abraham, Isaac and Israel, manifest your raw power to change all unfavourable situation confronting my children, in Jesus' name.

19. Every seed of witchcraft in my foundation and anointing of witchcraft in my family line, working to frustrate the endeavours of my children in life, I break your grip by the thunder of God, in the name of Jesus.

20. O Lord, let the joy, the peace and divine favour for my children be greatly multiplied and empower them to eat the labours of their hands, in the name of Jesus.

21. Satan, hear me and hear me well, my children will not reap evil harvest of their parents and will not pay the debt they did not owe, in the name of Jesus.

22. Every astral ball and magic mirror conjuring the face of any of my children in order to harvest their lives, lightening of God, break them to irreparable pieces, in the name of Jesus.

23. O Lord, let every satanic investment in the life of my children, be wasted and defend your own interest in their lives, in the name of Jesus.

24. Every yoke manufacturer delegated to harvest the life of my children, be exposed to open and double disgrace, in the name of Jesus.

25. Arrow of sudden and untimely death fired to harvest the destiny of my children, backfire, locate your owner and destroy your owner, in the name of Jesus.

26. Every power that has vowed to use any of my children to balance its account this year, you are a liar, I remove my children from your list of those sentenced to death by the blood of Jesus, in the name of Jesus.

27. Every satanic agent in my family line that has nominated any of my children for death this year, be substituted for my children's lives, in the name of Jesus.

28. Emptier, wasters and devourers of my father's house on assignment to vandalise the glory of my children, thunder of God destroy them, in the name of Jesus.

29. Every satanic court verdict upon the lives of my children at witchcraft coven, I overrule you by the blood of Jesus, backfire, in the name of Jesus.

30. I remove the names of my children from the book of failure and demonic side-track, in the name of Jesus.

31. Every spiritual hire killer/assassin on evil assignment to harvest any of my children, I cover my children with the blood of Jesus, therefore, carry your assignment back to your sender, in the name of Jesus.

32. Every conscious or unconscious covenant made on behalf of any of my children with the spirit of death and hell, fire of deliverance, break them, in the name of Jesus.

33. Every negative supernatural power pursuing my children to death, fire of vengeance pursue them and destroy them, in the name of Jesus.

34. Every evil ancestral law programmed into the genes of my children, be terminated now by the blood of Jesus, in the name of Jesus.

35. Sing this song as you wave the photograph of your first born.

    "In the name of Jesus, it is well, it is well....."

    In the name of Jesus, it is well, with my children.

36. Begin to thank the Lord for answered prayers.

14 THE GLORY OF MY CHILDREN MUST SHINE

Praise Worship

Bible Reading:- Isaiah 60:1-7

Confession

PRAYER POINTS

1. O Lord, the Kings of glory, fill the lives of my children with Your glory and make their glory a taboo and a poison for the enemies of their destiny, in the name of Jesus.

2. Father Lord, give unto my children grace and glory as you have created them for Your glory, in the name of Jesus.

3. Every power from the father's or mother's house planning to change the glory of my children to shame die, in the name of Jesus.

4. Lord Jesus, give unto my children power and glory that will renew their strength in the land of the living, in the name of Jesus.

5. Every strongman beholding the glory of my children for evil, angels of he living God, smite them with blindness, in the name of Jesus.

6. O God, let my children arise and shine as the glory of the Lord is risen upon them, in the name of Jesus.

7. My Father, arise for my children and let Your glory be seen upon them, in the name of Jesus.

8. As no one can cover the glory of the sun, the moon or the stars, any power planning to cover the glory of my children lightening and thunder of God strike them dead, in the name of Jesus.

9. I declare and decree that the brightness of the glory of my children will be like the glory of the sun, in the name of Jesus.

10. Any power planning to steal, kill or destroy the glory of my children, you are a liar, ground open and swallow them, in the name of Jesus.

11. O Lord, let the glory of my children promote their destiny and their quota of divine excellence, in the name of Jesus.

12. Lord Jesus, let the glory of my children be the star of their destiny and anointing for their greatness, in the name of Jesus.

13. O God my Father, let the last glory of my children be recovered and restored in many folds, in the name of Jesus.

14. O Lord, let Your glory upon my children be the mark of distinction upon their lives, in the name of Jesus.

15. Every power from the pit of hell planning that the glory of my children will sink and fade away, arrow of fire destroy them, in the name of Jesus.

16. Lord Jesus, let the glory of my children breakforth and attract high frame and honour of the powers of their father's house, in the name of Jesus.

17. The glory of my children shall not pass away unfulfilled but manifest and be held in high esteem, in the name of Jesus.

18. Every cloud of darkness covering the glory of my children, clear away by fire and let their glory burst into the open, in the name of Jesus.

19. You the glory of my children that has departed, wherever you are, appear now and begin to shine, in the name of Jesus.

20. I declare and I decree that the glory of my children will not die, their stars will not vanish; in this year blessing, honour, prosperity and favour will locate them, in the name of Jesus.

21. Every power, from the father's house, using the glory of my children to shine, your time is come, die, in the name of Jesus.

22. Sing this song 7 times as you wave the photographs of your children.

    I can see everything, turning around (3ce)

    For my children.

23. Begin to thank God for answered prayer.

15   OH LORD, POSITION AND PROMOTE MY CHILDREN FOR THEIR NEXT LEVEL

Praise Worship

Scripture Reading – Gen. 41:37-44; I Sam. 2:1-8, Dan. 3:26-30

Confession: Psalm 75:6-7; 113:7-8

PRAYER POINTS

1. By the power that promoted Joseph from the prison to the palace, O Lord, promote my children this year, in the name of Jesus.

2. Spirit of excellence that promoted Daniel, Hananiah, Mishael and Azariah, in the land of captivity, fall upon my children this year, in the name of Jesus.

3. As promotion comes not from the east or west, but from You, O Lord uplift my children in every area of their lives, in the name of Jesus.

4. O Lord my Father, uplift my children like eagle to the highest level and make them uncommon star in their generation, in the name of Jesus.

5. Every power of darkness issuing evil decree to militate against the desired promotion of my children, carry your evil load and die, in the name of Jesus.

6. Every evil chain of slavery, frustrating the chances of promotion for my children, break by fire and burn to ashes, in Jesus' name.

7. O Lord enlarge the coast of my children and uproot every root of stagnation to their promotion, in the name of Jesus.

8. Every satanic rope, tied around the advancement of my children to hinder their promotion, catch fire and burn to ashes, in the name of Jesus.

9. Favour of God, overshadow my children this year and lead them to their promotion, in the name of Jesus.

10. Every power sitting on the promotion of my children in their places of work, we withdraw your peace, your comfort and unseat you by fire, in the name of Jesus.

11. O God of increase and fruitfulness, let my children believing You for fruit of the womb, bring forth their own children this year by fire by force, in the name of Jesus.

12. O Lord, give new name to my children looking for job, promote them from applicant to employee and enter into their gainful employment, that will make them happy and comfortable in life, in the name of Jesus.

13. My Father, magnetize my single children by divine leading, to their rightful partner and be promoted from single to married this year, in the name of Jesus.

14. My children that are looking for placement in Higher Institution, receive your letter of admission without sweat to further your education this year, in the name of Jesus.

15. Every ancestral embargo, placed upon the promotion of my children, be revoked by the Blood of Jesus, in the name of Jesus.

16. Promotion, Progress and Success, you are the birth right of my children and their lives are waiting for you, manifest now, in the name of Jesus.

17. Spirit of promotion, wherever you are, appear and promote my children from zero level to hero and from ordinary to extra-ordinary, in the name of Jesus.

18. By the power that changed the story of Jabeez, O Lord, promote my children from Mr. Nobody to Mr. Somebody that is the most prominent in the father's house, in the name of Jesus.

19. Every evil mark of hatred and rejection that is affecting the timely promotion of my children, be rubbed off by the blood of Jesus, in the name of Jesus.

20. Every power assigned to kill the light of the glory of my children in order to amputate their promotion after the order of Shedrach, Meshback and Abednego, die, in the name of Jesus.

21. Anointing of late promotion, delayed promotion and overdue promotion, the destiny of my children is not for you, die, in Jesus' name.

22. You the hour of my children's promotion, appear now and put a new song in their mouth this year, in the name of Jesus.

23. I prophesy that, in this year, my children will leap into accelerated promotion and have reason to celebrate and jubilate, in the name of Jesus.

24. Foundational strongman from the father's house assigned to kill my children before their promotions appear, it is you that will die, die now without mercy, in the name of Jesus.

25. Every blood of animals or of human beings, shed by ancestral powers withholding the promotions of my children, loose your hold by the blood of Jesus, in the name of Jesus.

26. Every incense, candle, rituals and sacrifice prepared to terminate the promotion of my children, backfire and work against your owner, in the name of Jesus.

27. Divine helper that will promote the lives of my children, what are you still waiting or, manifest now, in the name of Jesus.

28. Every power of the Father's house fighting the future of my children at the edge of their promotion to the next level, ground open and swallow them, in the name of Jesus.

34. O God my Father, uphold and deliver my children from any death of a fool by mistake or error and cancel bad news or last minute tear over any of them, in the name of Jesus.

30. Lord Jesus, disappoint the devices of the crafty and expose the secret plans of household wickedness preventing my children from moving to their next level, in the name of Jesus.

31. Every star gazer, star hunters and star killers monitoring my children as they move into their next level, Angels of God smite them with blindness, in the name of Jesus.

32. Every stubborn enemy within the father's and mother's house of my children saying "No Way" for them to move to their next level, you are a liar, die your final death and enter into your grave, in the name of Jesus.

33. Every power that wants my children to remain stagnant like pool of water and end their lives in shame as a failure, thunder of God, destroy them, in the name of Jesus.

34. My Father, turn every disappointment of my children to fulfillment, move them from lamentation to laughter, take them from ridicule to glory and plug them to current of victory, in the name of Jesus.

35. You the habitation of darkness in the lives of my children preventing their moving to the next level, be permanently, desolate and wasted, in the name of Jesus.

36. Every area in the lives of my children in Satanic cage or bondage, hindering their moving forward in life, be released now by fire, in the name of Jesus.

37. O Lord, re-write the story of children, move them to their next level and make them center of attraction in their family line, in the name of Jesus.

38. Every plan of the enemy to make my children end their lives on the mockery avenue and arena of shame and disgrace, be nullified by the blood of Jesus and die, in the name of Jesus.

39. Lord Jesus, accelerates the season for uncommon laughter for my children and destroy every anti-testimony force targeting their laughter, in the name of Jesus.

40. O Lord, in the job, career, business and academics of my children, take them from the crowd and move them to their next level, in the name of Jesus.

41. My Father, as the year is going to an end, visit my children with blessings that cannot be doubted, miracles of how did it happen, joy unspeakable, uncommon mercy and abundance of grace, that will give them reason to celebrate, in the name of Jesus.

42. Lord Jesus, do not allow the enemies to celebrate the demotion of my children but make them to rise higher than where they were yesterday, in the name of Jesus.

43. My Father, my Father, my Father, anoint my children for sings, wonders and the miraculous that will make them a praise and a name in their father's house, in the name of Jesus.

44. Psalm 102:13 says – "Thou shalt arise and have mercy upon Zion, for the time to favour her, yea, the set time is come". According to Your Word, O Lord, let it be known that you will move my children from single to married, barren to mother of their own children, tenant to landlord and from job seeker to gainfully employed, in the name of Jesus.

45. Say "Thank You Jesus" seven (7) times

46. Shout seven (7) testimony receiving Hallelujah.

47. Sing this song 7 times as you wave their photographs to heaven.

    I can see everything turning around…

48. Begin to thank God for answered prayer.

16 MY CHILDREN SHALL BREAK FORTH AND BREAKTHROUGH IN LIFE

Praise Worship

Scripture Reading – Isaiah 32:15-20

Confession – Hosea 10:12

PRAYER POINTS

1. O God arise, break every wall of challenges and establish my children into their place of breakthroughs this year, in the name of Jesus.

2. Every evil supervision regulating the programmes of my children's lives, in order to frustrate their breakthroughs, die, in the name of Jesus.

3. Every breakthrough my children have seen in the dream, begin to manifest, after the order of Joseph, in the name of Jesus.

4. Every witchcraft battle, assigned against the moving forward of my children into their breakthroughs this year, backfire, in the name of Jesus.

5. Divine helpers, locate my children, the helpers that have departed, begin to reappear now for my children to break forth and breakthrough, in the name of Jesus.

6. Past failures and evil patterns of the father's house, you will not be repeated in the lives of my children to hinder their breakthroughs, in the name of Jesus.

7. O Lord, give my children your divine connection to those who will help them and push them into their breakthrough, in Jesus' name.
8. O Lord, provoke the destiny of my children to outstanding breakthroughs, perfection and fulfillment, in the name of Jesus.
9. Angels of the living God, roll away all stones of household wickedness and household witchcraft blocking the breakthroughs of my children, in the name of Jesus.
10. O Lord, reschedule my children into your agenda of breakthroughs and destroy every satanic clock and timetable working contrary to their destiny, in the name of Jesus.
11. By the power that called Lazarus out of the grave, I call out the buried breakthroughs of my children out of the grave by fire, manifest, in the name of Jesus.
12. Every power pressing sand, making rituals and sacrifices burning candles and incense in order to hold the breakthroughs of my children in bondage, die, in the name of Jesus.
13. You this year, co-operate with my children and catapult them from the valley of stagnancy to the mountain top of glorification, in the name of Jesus.
14. My father, let my children receive miracle of possible impossibility and breakforth into accelerated breakthroughs, in the name of Jesus.
15. You strongman of household wickedness and household witchcraft, saying that "it is finished" for my children and that they will not have testimony of breakthroughs in life, you are a liar, face yourselves, fight yourselves and destroy yourselves, in the name of Jesus.

16. As long as people can see the glory of the sun and the moon, O Lord, let my children enter into their breakthroughs and let their glory breakforth, in the name of Jesus.

17. Every power that is keeping my children low and working against their accelerated elevation, what do you think you are doing, die, in the name of Jesus.

18. I send confusion, disaster and chaos into the camp of evil arresters holding the breakthroughs of my children captive, in the name of Jesus.

19. Any dead relation sitting on the breakthroughs of my children be unseated by fire and release their physical and spiritual breakthroughs, in the name of Jesus.

20. O Lord, use the key You collected from Satan, when You triumphed on the cross, to open the cage, harboring the breakthroughs of my children, in the name of Jesus.

21. Every power that has formed covenant with death, in order to deny the entry of my children into their breakthroughs, by divine substitution, die in their place, in the name of Jesus.

22. Every destiny padlock, working against the breakthroughs of my children, Holy Ghost Fire, set them ablaze, in the name of Jesus.

23. You the breakthroughs of my children, your set time is come, therefore, breakforth in the name of Jesus. (Psalm 102:13)

24. O Lord, deliver my children from the old Prophet assigned to divert them from their place of breakthroughs, in the name of Jesus. (I Kings 13:11-31)

ANOINTED DESTINY CHANGING PRAYERS FOR YOUR CHILDREN

25. Every satanic weapon, fashioned against my children from the North, East, West and South, to prevent their journey into breakthroughs, backfire by fire, in the name of Jesus.

26. Every yoke of limitation and satanic embargo, operating around the breakthroughs of my children, break by fire, in the name of Jesus.

27. God of Elijah, revoke every covenant of disappointment at the edge of breakthroughs and empower my children to breakforth into explosive breakthroughs this year, in the name of Jesus.

28. Every problem in the background of my children, that is now in their foundation, working against their breakthroughs, receive divine solution, in the name of Jesus.

29. O God, open door of breakthroughs, that no man can shut for my children and let them break forth into their breakthroughs, in the name of Jesus.

30. Every Jericho wall, challenging the breakthroughs of my children, clear away at the shout of Seven Halleluyah, in the name of Jesus.

31. Every agent of darkness that established evil authority against the breakthroughs of my children, I command the sword of the Lord to rise against you and destroy you, in the name of Jesus.

32. O Lord my God, let Your overrunning flood seep away the habitation of the wicked strongman, attacking the progress of my children, to desolation, in the name of Jesus.

33. Begin to thank God for answered prayers.

OH LORD, RAISE DIVINE HELPERS FOR MY CHILDREN

Praise Worship

Bible Passage: Isaiah 41:10-20

Confession: Psalm 121:1-2

PRAYER POINTS

1. My children need helpers O Lord, raise divine helpers for them, in the name of Jesus.

2. You the helpers of my children that have disappeared, wherever you are, appear now, in the name of Jesus.

3. I withdraw the peace, the joy and comfort of the helpers assigned for my children until they arise to help them, in the name of Jesus.

4. In all endeavours of my children in life, helpers shall not be far from them, in the name of Jesus.

5. My children lift up their eyes unto You, O Lord, arise for their help and let them not be put to shame, in the name of Jesus.

6. O Lord You are the help of the helpless and very present help in time of trouble, manifest in the situations of my children, in the name of Jesus.

7. As my children go up and down on earth, let them meet that man/woman that will help them and bless them, in the name of Jesus.

ANOINTED DESTINY CHANGING PRAYERS FOR YOUR CHILDREN

8. O Lord send help from Zion to my children to complete all their uncompleted projects, in the name of Jesus.

9. Where is the Lord God of Elijah, arise and help my children to break every yoke of late marriage or no marriage that is making them unhappy, in the name of Jesus.

10. O Lord my God, raise a voice and intercessors for my children concerning their delayed and denied promotion to be speedily released unto them, in the name of Jesus.

11. Lord Jesus, let mercy speak for my children, let help arise from the four corners of the world and give them turn around breakthroughs, in the name of Jesus.

12. Father Lord, connect my children to divine helpers that will help them to get a job that will make them comfortable in life, in the name of Jesus.

13. You powers of the Fathers house driving away helpers from locating my children, what are you still living for, die, in the name of Jesus.

14. As the boys look unto face of their fathers and the girls look unto the hand of their mothers, so do my children lift up their eyes unto You, O Lord, God, arise for their help this year, in the name of Jesus.

15. By all the powers by which You are God, O Lord direct my children to the helpers that their miracles have been waiting for, in the name of Jesus.

16. Every veil preventing my children from seeing and meeting their man with a jar, that will help them, catch fire and burn to ashes, in the name of Jesus.

17. I prophecy unto the lives of my children that their marriage shall not fail and their helpers shall not die, in the name of Jesus.

18. O God arise and quicken the steps of my children's helpers to their destination, in the name of Jesus.

19. Sing this song 7 times with rejoicing

    Gbe 'ranwodide, JesuOluwa

    Lonaara, l'onaiyanu

    Fawonomo mi

18 MY CHILDREN WILL REACH THEIR GOAL

Praise Worship

Scripture Reading – Gen. 45:1-12

Confession: Deut. 1:8

PRAYER POINTS

1. Every Red Sea on the way of my children to their promised, land, divide, in the name of Jesus. (Exod. 14:21-22)
2. Every wall of Jericho hindering my children from getting to their promised land, fall down flat, in the name of Jesus. (Joshua 7:20)
3. Every stubborn Pharaoh of the Father's house, stubbornly pursuing my children on the way to their promised land, perish in your Red Sea, in the name of Jesus.
4. Power of demotion, following my children about, to hinder them from reaching their goal in life, die, in the name of Jesus.
5. Any power that needs to die for my children to reach their goal, it is time for you to die, die now, in the name of Jesus.
6. Every closed door leading to my children's entry into their promised land, hear the Word of the Lord, open now by fire, in the name of Jesus.
7. O Lord, set in disarray, any plan of the enemy targeted to frustrate my children from reaching their goal, in the name of Jesus.

8. O Lord my Father, anything You need to do for my children to reach their goal and rewrite the history of their family, do it now, in the name of Jesus.

9. Destiny diverters and detractors, assigned to frustrate my children in their journey to the Promised Land and reach their goal, die by fire, in the name of Jesus.

10. O Lord, give my children the spirit of Caleb and Joshua, to surmount every opposition and giant on their way to enter the Promised Land and reach their goal, in the name of Jesus.

11. Lord Jesus, empower my children to reach their promised land so as to become relevant, sort out and most prominent in their Father's house, in the name of Jesus.

12. Every spiritual robber, trailing my children in order to truncate their journey to the Promise Land, receive bullet of fire and die, in the name of Jesus.

13. My Father, put upon my children, divine bullet proof against the weapons of the enemy, designed to cut short their journey to the Promised Land and reach their goal, in the name of Jesus.

14. Every problem and obstacle that will stop my children from reaching their goal, catch fire, in the name of Jesus.

15. O Lord, let You covenant of Long life, be established in the lives of my children, so that they will reach their goal in the land of the living, in the name of Jesus.

16. Host of heaven, arrest and persecute the satanic forces, delegated to stop my children from reaching their goal, in the name of Jesus.

17. Every power prolonging the journey of my children, to reach their goal and fulfill their destiny in life, I place judgement of death upon you, die, in the name of Jesus.

18. Angels of mercy, favour and blessing, overshadow the lives of my children, until they enter their promised land and reach their goal, in the name of Jesus.

19. Every agenda of failure imagine, planned or programmed to hinder my children from reaching their goal, die, in the name of Jesus.

20. Every Pharaoh, that will not let my children go easily, to pursue their journey to the Promised Land and reach their goal, die a shameful death, in the name of Jesus.

21. Every arrow of untimely death, fired at my children, to terminate their journey to the Promised Land, backfire, in the name of Jesus.

22. Destiny wasters and destroyers, hear me and hear me well, you will not be able to perform your enterprise over my children not to reach their goal, in the name of Jesus.

23. Power of resurrection, quicken my children's mortal body, increase their faith and wisdom to start well and finish well when they reach their goal, in the name of Jesus.

24. Joseph reached his goal, Ruth reached her goal, Jesus reached His goal, by the same covenant of achievement, all my children will reach their goal in grand style, in the name of Jesus.

25. Agent of sorrow and sadness, programmed against the purposeful journey of my children to their promised land, die, in the name of Jesus.

26. Paralyzing wind blowing to paralyze the passion and zeal of my children to reach their goal, hear the word of the Lord, "Be still", in the name of Jesus.

27. In this year, O Lord my Father, turn back the captivity of my children, comfort them on all sides and increase their greatness to superlative degree, in the name of Jesus.

28. You this year, before you go, deliver all the denied and delayed job, business, contract, pregnancy, admission, promotion, marriage and good health to my children, in the name of Jesus.

29. Spirit of Pisgah, delegated by powers of the father's house, to hinder my children from entering their promised land, die, in the name of Jesus.

30. I prophesy into the lives of my children that they will reach their goal with joy and become international celebrities, in the name of Jesus.

31. Sing this song seven (7) times

    My children shall reach their promised Land (2ce)

    Whether their enemies like or not

    My children shall reach their promised land.

32. Begin to thank Go for answered prayers.

19 O LORD PERFECT EVERYTHING THAT CONCERNS MY CHILDREN

Praise Worship

Bible Reading – Psalm 138

Confession: Psalm 138:8

PRAYER POINTS

1. O God of perfection, put your seal of perfection on everything that concerns my children and let the story of their lives change, in the name of Jesus.

2. O God of perfection, let every curse and covenant of failure in the lives of my children break by the blood of Jesus, in the name of Jesus.

3. Everything remaining for the joy of my children to be full and overflowing, O Lord, perfect it, in the name of Jesus.

4. Every BUT in the lives of my children, that is causing them reproach and sorrow, O Lord, remove it, in the name of Jesus.

5. God of possibility, make possible, everything the enemy thinks is impossible in the lives of my children, in the name of Jesus.

6. God of suddenly, arise suddenly in the lives of my children and push them into their all-round, turn-around breakthrougs, in the name of Jesus.

7. God of surprises, arise suddenly and pleasantly surprise my children with the miracle of "how did it happen", in Jesus name.

ANOINTED DESTINY CHANGING PRAYERS FOR YOUR CHILDREN

8. By the wonder of Your power, O Lord, do the unusual and unexpected in the lives of my children, that will make their enemies to wonder in amazement, in the name of Jesus.

9. Any covenant made with the ground, with any evil tree, with any body of river, against any of my children, break by fire and backfire in the name of Jesus.

10. All the helpers of my children that have disappeared, by the decree of heaven, begin to reappear and favour them, in the name of Jesus.

11. You the marriage of my children, receive honey and new wine and begin to experience intimate relationship in Jesus' name.

12. You the business of my children, receive anointing of increase and profitability in this month, in the name of Jesus.

13. Every uncompleted project of my children, receive anointing of perfection, fulfillment and completion, after the order of Zerubbabel, in the name of Jesus.

14. I decree by the decree of heaven that there will be a change in the lives of my children from failure to success, disappointment to divine appointment, barrenness to fruitfulness, poverty to prosperity, sorrow to joy and Mr. Nobody to Mr. Somebody great, in the name of Jesus.

15. O God of Jabez, cloth my children with fresh honour and enlarge their coasts, in the name of Jesus.

16. Every unfavourable situation in the lives of my children, that is causing them shame and sorrow, your time is up, receive divine change now, in the name of Jesus.

17. O Lord, let the names of my children capture prosperity and cause sleepless night for all those who will help them, until they do it, in the name of Jesus.

18. Every curse of stagnation and journey to backwardness programmed into the lives of my children, to hinder their moving forward, your time is up, backfire, in the name of Jesus.

19. O Lord, order the steps of my children to concide with favour, mercy and goodness, in the name of Jesus.

20. O Lord, by the power that elevated Joseph, let my children be elevated to fulfill their divine destiny, in the name of Jesus.

21. O God that changes times and seasons, change every unwanted situation the lives of my children and let them have unspeakable life changing experience, in the name of Jesus.

22. Every evil mandate given to any power to supervise the life and family of my children, I reverse it by fire, in the name of Jesus.

23. In this year, O Lord perfect all the good things you started in the lives of my children and let all disappointments of the past become divine appointment, in the name of Jesus.

24. O Lord my God, let Your perfect peace begin to rule and reign in the troubled areas of the lives of my children and let the siege be over, in the name of Jesus.

25. Every good thing that has to do with the lives of my children, receive anointing of perfection for divine perfection, in the name of Jesus.

26. Every power of the father's house that has acquired witchcraft power because of my children, use the power to destroy yourself, in the name of Jesus.

27. Begin to praise the Lord for answered prayers.

BLOOD OF JESUS, SPEAK FOR MY CHILDREN

Praise Worship

(a) There is power, power, wonder working power

(b) There is power, there is power, there is power in the blood

(c) There is power mighty in the blood (2ce)

(d) O the Blood of Jesus (3ce) it washes white as now

(e) The Blood of Jesus, the blood that conquered Satan

Bible Reading: Gen 4:9-12

Confession: Exod. 12:13

PRAYER POINTS

1. Blood of Jesus, raise a voice and speak for my children among the crowd to be sort out for in the name of Jesus.

2. Every good thing in the lives of my children, that is dead or about to die, receive the resurrection power of Jesus and come alive, in the name of Jesus.

3. I raise the Blood of Jesus and declare by the decree of heaven against all wicked powers, that do not want my children to go, release them and let them go to prosper, in the name of Jesus.

4. Blood of Jesus, speak solution to the barren situation of my children, heal their womb and make them become proud mother of their own children, in the name of Jesus.

5. Blood of Jesus, speak destruction to the powers of darkness causing marital delays for my children, break the yoke of late marriage, magnetize them to their rightful partners and make them evidence of Your unchanging power, in the name of Jesus.

6. Blood of Jesus, erase every negative recognition and nullify, every evil identification marks, placed upon the lives of my children, to hinder their breakthroughs and set their lives on cause for signs, wonders and testimony, in the name of Jesus.

7. I draw a circle of the blood of Jesus around my children, for protection from sudden, untimely death, accident, tragedy, mishap and disaster. It shall not be their portion, in the name of Jesus.

8. By the power in the Blood of Jesus, I curse the root of every work of darkness, operating in the lives of my children, wither and die, in the name of Jesus.

9. Every destructive carry over from the family line of my children, to hinder their testimony in life, blood of Jesus kill them, in the name of Jesus.

10. Any powers trying to reject my children from their inherited promise land, blood of Jesus expose them to open and double disgrace, in the name of Jesus.

11. Blood of Jesus nullify the binding effects of all unholy baths, evil vision, satanic prophecy and hidden covenants, programmed into the lives of my children by false prophets, in white garment churches, in the name of Jesus.

12. Every wicked law and evil word, programmed against the day, star, destiny, future and lives of my children, in the sun and the

moon, blood of Jesus frustrate them, they shall not be established, in the name of Jesus.

13. Every negative of stagnation and season of failure in the circle of the sun, and the moon, against my children, blood of Jesus, blot them out, in the name of Jesus.

14. Any power that wants me to bury any of my children, blood of Jesus pursue them to die their final death and locate their own grave, in the name of Jesus.

15. Every satanic certificate of ownership and occupancy over the lives of my children, be revoked by the blood of Jesus, in the name of Jesus.

16. Every satanic embargo over the certificate, womb, marriage, business, project, health, helpers, and lives of my children, be lifted by the blood of Jesus, in the name of Jesus.

17. I release my children with the blood of Jesus from the binding effects of every collective, inherited, ancestral and acquired curses and covenants, from both sides of their family line, in the name of Jesus.

18. Every information about my children, present in the any satanic altar and data bank and secrets in possession of evil monitoring agents, I withdraw them by fire and by the blood of Jesus, in the name of Jesus.

19. When the host of household wickedness and household witchcraft shall come like a flood, to encamp around and against my children, blood of Jesus, arise to defend, deliver and preserve them and let there be evil war in the camp of the enemy, in the name of Jesus.

20. Blood of Jesus, purge the foundation of my children and use them to rewrite the history of their family, in the name of Jesus.

21. Blood of Jesus, frustrate the tokens of the enemy, let your protective power overshadow my children, so that Satan will not use them to balance his account, in the name of Jesus.

22. I raise the Blood of Jesus against the stubborn strongman, that wants my children to die before the day of their glory and honour, in the name of Jesus.

23. Every negative handwriting, in the circle of the sun and the moon, designed against the destiny of my children, I cancel you with the blood of Jesus, in the name of Jesus.

24. Any wicked power placing witchcraft legs on the wall, in order to attend coven meeting because of my children, I challenge you with the Blood of Jesus, sleep the sleep of death and die, in the name of Jesus.

25. Blood of Jesus, erase every negative record of the past, about the lives of my children and begin a new dimension of wonders in their lives, in the name of Jesus.

26. Blood of Jesus, erase all unprofitable marks of hatred and rejection, placed upon my children and cover it with the marks of attraction and acceptance, in the name of Jesus.

27. Every evil association and unfriendly friends that pulled my children backward last year, be separated by the blood of Jesus and die, in the name of Jesus.

28. I speak destruction by the blood of Jesus to the root of every embarrassing situation and circumstances in the lives of my children, in the name of Jesus.

29. Every voice from the mortuary/grave, inviting my children, I raise the blood of Jesus against you, die and rise no more, in the name of Jesus.

30. Blood of Jesus, poison the root of problems in the foundation of my children, and let their problems begin to have problems, in the name of Jesus.

31. Every blood poured on the ground to establish covenant of death against my children, power in the Blood of Jesus, arise and revoke it, in the name of Jesus.

32. By the power in the Blood of Jesus, I destroy the evil alignment, between household witchcraft and household wickedness, to waste the destiny of my children, in the name of Jesus.

33. Begin to thank God for answer prayers.

21 MY CHILDREN WILL EXCEL IN LIFE

Praise Worship

Scripture Reading: Daniel 5:10-17

Confession: Daniel 6:3

PRAYER POINTS

1. Anointing of excellence, spirit of intelligence; divine vision, knowledge and understanding for accelerated progress, fall upon my children, in the name of Jesus.

2. Every door of excellence, that the enemy has closed against my children, hear the word of the Lord, open by fire, in the name of Jesus.

3. O Lord, plant the seed of excellence in the lives of my children that will make them excel among their equals, in the name of Jesus.

4. Excellent spirit, incubate the lives of my children, for accelerated advancement in their studies and business, in the name of Jesus.

5. Every imprisoned and buried potentials, hindering excellent spirit in the lives of my children, be released by the thunder fire, in the name of Jesus.

6. Excellent spirit that came upon Daniel to reveal the secret things, fall upon my children, in the name of Jesus.

7. Excellence spirit, power for excellence, the lives of my children are available for you, enter, in the name of Jesus.

8. Every anti-progress altar fashioned against excellent spirit in the lives of my children, catch fire and burn to ashes, in the name of Jesus.

9. Anointing to excel, power to progress and grace to prosper, fall mightily upon every area and department of my children's lives, in the name of Jesus.

10. Where the Babylonian magicians failed, let the excellent spirit after the order of Daniel incubate my children to achieve excellence, in the name of Jesus.

11. O Lord, open the eyes and ears of my children and make them instruments of divine revelation, to key into the spirit of excellence, in the name of Jesus.

12. As Daniel received excellent spirit and enjoyed favour and promotion, O Lord give unto my children excellent spirit, accelerated promotion and divine favour in the name of Jesus.

13. I speak confusion/frustration into the mist of every evil gathering, taking place because of my children, planning to overturn the excellent spirit in their lives, in the name of Jesus.

14. My children, I prophesy into your lives that, because of the excellent spirit of God in your lives, your future shall be wonderful, your lives shall end in bliss and not in shame, the glory of your lives shall shine and your end shall be better than your beginning, in the name of Jesus.

15. Every evil competitor that is jealous of the excellent spirit in the lives of my children and planning evil for them, I command their plans to backfire, in the name of Jesus.

16. Every power of the Father's house planning to return my children to square one and zero level, because of the excellent spirit in their lives, you are a liar, receive sword of destruction and die, in the name of Jesus.

17. Every evil cord of wickedness, sin or iniquity, blocking excellent spirit from my children, be cut off by the sword of fire, in the name of Jesus.

18. Every spiritual barrier and demonic limitation to the advancement of my children, be dismantled by thunder from heaven, in the name of Jesus.

19. I break with the blood of Jesus, the curse of evil ritual and covenant, affecting the progress of my children, in the name of Jesus.

20. My Father, let bad times and evil seasons change in the life of my children, baptize them with rains of favour, and let doors of favour open to them, in the name of Jesus.

21. Every river of regret and sorrow, programmed by the enemy, to flow into the lives of my children, dry up by fire, in the name of Jesus.

22. Every destructive habit in the lives of my children, assigned to make them candidates of hell fire, die, in Jesus' name.

23. Every power planning to uproot my children from their garden of breakthroughs, I command your plans to backfire, in the name of Jesus.

24. Divine wisdom, knowledge and understanding, incubate the lives of my children for excellence, in the name of Jesus.

25. Every curse of "Thou shall not excel" placed upon my children by the strongman of their father's house, break and backfire, in the name of Jesus.

26. O Lord my Father, as you gave wisdom to Solomon, understanding to Daniel and knowledge to Joseph, repeat these blessings in the lives of my children for excellence, in the name of Jesus.

27. Lord Jesus, let the destiny of my children be reconciled to the agenda of heaven, far divine elevation, in the name of Jesus.

28. Sudden and untimely death, assigned to kill excellent spirit in the lives of my children, go back to your sender, in the name of Jesus.

29. I declare and I decree, no power will stop my children, they shall excel in life, in the name of Jesus.

30. Begin to thank God for answered prayers

22 MY CHILDREN MUST SUCCEED

Praise Worship

Scripture Reading – Joshua 1:1-9

Confession – Gen. 39: 3

PRAYER POINTS

1. You my children, jump out from the valley of failure into the camp of success, in the name of Jesus.
2. Every witchcraft wall of Jericho surrounding the success of my children, I pull you down with the shout of Halleluyah, in the name of Jesus. (Shout 7 Halleluyahs very loud)
3. My children, receive deliverance from the spirit of minimal achievement, in the name of Jesus.
4. O Lord, magnetise my children to success, magnetise success to them, and let every fountain of failure, flowing into their lives, dry up now, in the name of Jesus.
5. Lord Jesus, launch the feet of my children into renewed and greater opportunities for success and paralyse all opportunity wasters, in the name of Jesus.
6. You my children, whether the devil likes it or not, you will not die a failure, in the name of Jesus.
7. Failure, fail in the lives of my children, in the name of Jesus.
8. Every strongman from the father's house, withholding key of

success from my children, enough is enough, release the key and die, in the name of Jesus.

9. You the spirit of success, come upon my children now and let the beauty of God be seen in their lives, in the name of Jesus.

10. Thou power of God, upgrade the brain of my children, for excellent performance in their academic pursuits, in the name of Jesus.

11. Every limiting power of demotion, from my children's family line, your time is up, die, in the name of Jesus.

12. Every barrier to success in the lives of my children, caterpillar of heaven, bulldoze them, in the name of Jesus.

13. Every anti-success marks, placed on my children by the stubborn strongman, blood of Jesus, wipe them off, in the name of Jesus.

14. Divine success, overshadow my children now and let their stars begin to shine brighter, in the name of Jesus.

15. Every door of success, that the enemy has closed against any of my children, open now by fire, in the name of Jesus

16. Divine success, locate my children, re-write their story and let them become a success story in life, in the name of Jesus.

17. All my children going for job interview shall receive divine success and favour for excellent performance, in the name of Jesus.

18. Divine success locate the business and academic pursuits of my children and let them breakthrough into unimaginable success, in the name of Jesus.

19. O God my Father, position my children for uncommon success and make their lives a wonder and a testimony, in the name of Jesus.

20. Every household witchcraft monitoring the success of my children, Angels of the Living God, smite them with blindness, in the name of Jesus.

21. O Lord, let my children pluck the seed of success in everything they lay their hands upon, in the name of Jesus.

22. Father Lord, place the key of success into the hands of my children and let their lives experience divine acceleration, in the name of Jesus.

23. O Lord my Father, initiate my children into the club of the successful and grant unto them the success that will announce them to the world, in the name of Jesus.

24. O Lord God of Israel, promote the lives of my children to advertise your glory, in the name of Jesus.

25. Holy Spirit, equip my children with wisdom, knowledge and understanding to be successful in all areas of their lives, in the name of Jesus.

26. O Lord, let every mountain-like problems in the lives of my children, become their stepping stone and pedestal to their success, to record great success, in the name of Jesus.

27. Every curse of failure pronounced upon my children, blood of Jesus, nullify them and convert them to outstanding success; in the name of Jesus.

28. Divine success, the lives of my children are available for you, manifest by fire, in the name of Jesus.

29. My children need change, O Lord, change them with Your power of change and let them succeed in life, in the name of Jesus.

30. Begin to thank God for answered prayers.

23 NAME OF JESUS, SPEAK FOR MY CHILDREN

Praise and Worship

Bible Reading: Phil. 2:5-11

Confession: Isaiah 9:6

PRAYER POINTS

1. Raise up the photographs of your children and wave them to heaven as you sing

    i. That wonderful name, Jesus (3ce) There is no other name I know.

    ii. His name is higher, than any other name, His name is Jesus, His name is Lord.

    iii. Jesus is a mighty God, every power bow before Him, He is a mighty God.

    iv. At the mention of Jesus, every knee shall bow......

    v. When Jesus says 'Yes' nobody can say 'No' (2ce) up, up Jesus, down, down satan.

    vi. Jesus is the sweetest name I know.....

    vii. I know His name (2ce) His name is (Wonderful, Comforter, Prince of Peace, Mighty God, Everlasting Father)

2. Raise up the photographs of your children and wave them to heaven as you sing.
   i. Alagbaral'Olorun mi, alagbaraniJesu mi......
   ii. Mo mop'alagbaraniJesu mi, O lagbaralatis'etoaiye mi
   iii. Agbara Baba ka a o, agbaraJesuka (2ce) Gbogboisoro to walaiye mi o....
   iv. Jesulowo Re lo wa, Baba lowo Re lo wa, agbara, gbogboagbarapatapata
   v. Jesu je Alagbara (2ce) AgbaratiSataniko to tiJesurara
   vi. Ijinle, olorukonla, orukoJesu lo kariaiye.

3. Jesus, Your name is Wonderful, by the wonders of Your name; perform Your wonderful wonder in the lives of my children, that will make their enemies to wonder in amazement, in the name of Jesus.

4. Jesus, Your name is Comforter, by the comfort of Your name, comfort my children on all sides, enlarge their coasts and let tears of sorrow dry up, in the name of Jesus.

5. Sing this songs and pray the prayer
   i. You are the Mighty God, the great I am, Halleluyah (2ce)
   ii. Kos'agbara to dabitiJesu..........................

   Jesus, Your name is Mighty God, let every knee of barrenness, joblessness, academic failure, marital delay, career stagnancy, in the lives of my children, bow and die, in the name of Jesus.

ANOINTED DESTINY CHANGING PRAYERS FOR YOUR CHILDREN

6. Jesus, Your name is Prince of Peace, let Your perfect peace, give my children peace always, and by all means, to begin to rule and reign in every troubled area of their lives and bring them to haven of peaceful rest, in the name of Jesus.

7. Name of Jesus, speak for my children,

i. Let the heavens of my children open to fresh outpour of early and later rain of supernatural abundance.

    ii. Let heavens rewrite the story of my children and restore their captivity, that wicked powers of their father's house have stolen.

    iii. Let them experience healing anointing, that will terminate every terminal disease and sickness in their lives.

    iv. Let their virtues and beneficial potentials in the prison house of Satan, be released by thunder and by fire.

    v. Let them enjoy financial turn-around that will put an end to lack, poverty and yoke of debt in their lives.

    vi. Let them experience divine acceleration from the valley of stagnancy to the mountain top of glorification.

    vii. Let them arise, begin to shine in the comfort of unusual, and uncommon breakthroughs.

    viii. Let Your resurrection power revive every dry bone situation in their lives.

    ix. Let the power that pulled down the wall of Jericho dismantle satanic roadblock mounted by the wicked strongman of the father's house on their way of progress.

x. Let every Red Sea situation, receive divine divide, to enable them move into their promised land.

xi. Let their past disappointments turn to divine appointment at the appointed time.

xii. Let Your power that knows no impossibility, arise suddenly and do the impossible, the uncommon and the unusual for them.

xiii. Let Satanic embargo, energizing yoke of delay and denial, be cleared away by caterpillar of heaven.

xiv. Let every covenant of death, programmed by Satan to harvest the lives of my children, break by fire and backfire, in the name of Jesus.

xv. Let every power, working against divine agenda to hinder, delay and cancel the promises of God for them, die their final death and locate their grave, in the name of Jesus.

xvi. Let Your anointing of perfection perfect every good thing You commenced in their lives and do it to perfection, in the name of Jesus.

xvii. Let failure fail in their lives and re-enroll them in the school of success, in the name of Jesus.

xviii. Pour Your oil upon them, heal their root, anoint their destiny afresh and empower them to reach their goal in life, in the name of Jesus.

xix. Let every power attacking their divine helpers, receive judgement of sudden and untimely death, in the name of Jesus.

xx. Do not allow them to live in shame, die in shame and live a wasted life in hell fire, in the name of Jesus.

xxi. Let every household wickedness and household witchcraft sitting on their benefits and holding them in bondage, be unseated by fire and die now, in the name of Jesus.

xxii. Let their blessings that have missed the road, come back now, locate them and settle down with them, in the name of Jesus.

8. Sing this song seven (7) times

   The name, The name of Jesus,

   Is greater, and higher than all names,

   It is not an ordinary name,

   It's a name that's full of power and praise

9. Begin to thank God for answered prayers.

24 MY JOY OVER MY CHILDREN SHALL BE FULL

Praise Worship

Scripture Reading – Jer. 31:11-13; Isaiah 35:10; Isaiah 51:11

Confession – Prov. 23:24

PRAYER POINTS

1. My children will not run from their joy and their joy will not run from them, in the name of Jesus.

2. O Lord, let the joy of the enemy over the lives of my children be turned to baptism of sorrow, in the name of Jesus.

3. Every power delegated to spoil the joy of my children and cause them sorrow and mourning, I terminate your joy by the blood of Jesus, in the name of Jesus.

4. Father Lord, turn the mourning of my children into dancing, remove their sackcloth and cloth them with joy unspeakable, in the name of Jesus.

5. O Lord God Almighty, suffocate every power of sorrow in the lives of children, turn their sorrow into joy, put laughter in their mouth and dancing in their feet, in the name of Jesus.

6. O Lord my Father, consume every garment of sorrow in the lives of my children, clothe them with garments of comfort and rejoicing, and let song of glory, victory and praises continually be in their mouth, in the name of Jesus.

7. Holy Ghost Fire, dry up every fountain of perpetual sorrow and uncontrollable tears in the lies of my children, in the name of Jesus.

8. I reject the spirit of heaviness for my children. Anything that will not allow the joy of the Lord to flow in their lives, fall down and die, in the name of Jesus.

9. I refuse to wear garment of tribulation, sorrow and shame over my children. Every evil arrow fired to hold their lives in bondage, backfire, in the name of Jesus.

10. I cancel with the blood of Jesus, every appointment with sorrow and tragedy; it shall not be the portion of my children, in the name of Jesus.

11. Every good thing that remains for you to do, to make the joy of my children full and complete, O God my Father, do it now before the end of this year, in the name of Jesus.

12. O Lord, give my children a turn-around breakthrough that will disgrace the Goliath of their joy and sink the Pharaoh of their comfort in the Red Sea, in the name of Jesus.

13. O Lord, let the event that will promote me and make me a proud father/mother, happen in the lives of my children, in the name of Jesus.

14. On my children's day of joy, honour and glory, I shall not be represented and people will not rise one minutue silence for me, in the name of Jesus.

15. Any power from the Father's house, wishing my children to die before their day of joy and honour, it is you that will die, die now, in the name of Jesus.

16. Any ancestral power assigned against my children to live and die unfulfilled, and uncelebrated, you are a liar, die a shameful death, in the name of Jesus.

17. Every appointment with the mortuary and cemetery because of any of my children, I cancel it with the blood of Jesus, in the name of Jesus.

18. I shall not bury any of my children and my labour over their lives shall not be in vain. I am the one that will eat the fruit of my labour, and my labour shall not be in vain, in the name of Jesus.

19. Whether the devil likes it or not, the day of joy of my children will come and people will gather to rejoice with them, in the name of Jesus.

20. The joy of the Lord shall be the strength of my children to soar higher like eagle into grace and glory, in the name of Jesus.

21. Ancestral evil pattern of failure, defeat and stagnancy shall not prosper in the lives of my children, in the name of Jesus.

22. Arrow of sorrow, plantation of sadness, operating in the lives of my children, jump out by fire and locate your owner, in Jesus name.

23. The rivers of joy springing in the lives of my children shall never dry up but continue to flow to overflowing, in the name of Jesus.

24. Lord Jesus, let there be outpouring of oil of gladness upon the head of my children, that will heal their roots, catapult them into the limelight and advertise their joy in the name Jesus.

25. Every warfare, prepared against the peace of my children and every design of the enemy to turn their jubilation to lamentation, be frustrated by fire, in the name of Jesus.

26. Everything causing me joy will not cause me sorrow over my children, I shall not die but live to see my children fulfilled in life and share in their joy, in the name of Jesus.

27. O God of Isaac, arise in Your power, take my children from the crowd and give them special blessings in their marital life that will turn their mourning to dancing and their sorrow to joy, in the name of Jesus.

28. My joy shall know no boundary over my children, as they record outstanding successes in life, in the name of Jesus.

29. Joy unspeakable, baptize my children before the end of this year, and let every chaos turn to chorus of joy, in the name of Jesus.

30. O Lord, let the season of uncommon joy that will provoke weeping for joy, begin to manifest in the lives of my children and make me a living witness, in the name of Jesus.

31. Lord Jesus, let those who saw my children and pitied their tears, witness their season of unspeakable joy and weep for joy with them, in the name of Jesus.

32. I cancel bad news and sorrow concerning my children, I loose good news, open heavens and new open doors, that will make their joy full and complete, in the name of Jesus.

33. Begin to thank the Lord for answered prayers.

25 MY CHILDREN WILL FULFIL THEIR DESTINY

Praise Worship

Scripture Reading – Isaiah 15:4-9

Confession – Isaiah 51:11

PRAYER POINTS

1. You the destiny of my children, arise by fire, and move forward into signs and wonder, in the name of Jesus.

2. You the destiny of my children, receive the touch of God, arise and enter into your breakthroughs, in the name of Jesus.

3. Every power calling the name and the head of my children for evil, in order to do them evil, thunder fire of God, answer them and destroy them, in the name of Jesus.

4. Every stubborn household enemy, delegated to bury the destiny of my children, ground open and swallow them, in the name of Jesus.

5. Every arrow of wickedness and destruction, targeted against the destiny of my children, you will not locate them, locate your owner and destroy your owner, in the name of Jesus.

6. Every spirit of antichrist, pursuing the lives of my children to hell fire, die by fire, in the name of Jesus.

7. Every seed of failure, planted in the lives of my children to disgrace destroy their destiny, catch fire and burn to ashes, in Jesus name.

8. Every power, seeking for revenge on my children, for the sins of their parent, in order to destroy their destiny, receive sword of destruction and die, in the name of Jesus.

9. Every witchcraft in my foundation, rebelling against my children, loose your hold and die, in the name of Jesus.

10. Every curse or covenant in my foundation working against the destiny of my children, blood of Jesus, break and destroy them, in the name of Jesus.

11. You my children's destiny, refuse to harbor bewitchment, in the name of Jesus.

12. I break every generational curses and collective family captivity over the lives of my children by the blood of Jesus, in the name of Jesus.

13. Every door/gate the enemy has closed against the destiny of my children, hear the Word of the Lord, Ephrata, be opened now to success and breakthroughs, in the name of Jesus.

14. Every spiritual death sentence, passed on my children, be reversed by the blood of Jesus, In the name of Jesus.

15. Every covenant of delay and denial militating against the destiny of my children, expire now, in the name of Jesus.

16. Every witchcraft utterances and projection against the destiny of my children, be nullified by the blood of Jesus and backfire, in the name of Jesus.

17. Every satanic vehicle, transporting the blessings of my children to demonic market for sale, crash-land catch fire and burn to ashes, in the name of Jesus.

18. You the destiny of my children, that the enemy is holding in bondage, jump out by fire, arise and shine, in the name of Jesus.

19. Every stubborn witchcraft, holding the lives of my children captive, I raise Blood of Jesus against you, release them now or die, in the name of Jesus.

20. Anything in the lives of my children, that is making them to hate God, and hate the Word of God, your time is up, die, in the name of Jesus.

21. Every foundation of witchcraft and familiar spirit in the lives of my children, blood of Jesus destroy them, in the name of Jesus.

22. You the evil pattern of premature death in my family line, break and release my children, in the name of Jesus.

23. Every mirror of darkness, monitoring the destiny of my children, thunder fire of God, break them to pieces, in the name of Jesus.

24. Every caldron of darkness harbouring the virtue and the potentials of my children, hammer of God, break them to pieces, in the name of Jesus.

25. Every foundational, inherited and collective curses/covenant working to destroy the colourful destiny of my children, break by the blood of Jesus, in the name of Jesus.

26. Every power at the gate of death, killing good things in the lives of my children, somersault and die, in the name of Jesus.

27. Lord Jesus, frustrate all satanic decisions taken at evil witchcraft covens concerning the destiny of my children, in the name of Jesus.

28. O Lord my God, renew your covenant of mercy, favour and blessing over the destiny of my children, in the name of Jesus.

29. Every padlock of darkness locking up good things away from my children, Holy Ghost fire, set them ablaze, in the name of Jesus.
30. Every bewitchment and enchantment, programmed into the destiny of my children, backfire by fire, in the name of Jesus.
31. Any habit in the lives of my children that will destroy their destiny and bring shame and disgrace to the family, Holy Spirit, kill them, in the name of Jesus.
32. Lord Jesus, uproot the operation and power of delay, preventing my children from entering into their breakthroughs, in the name of Jesus.
33. Every power assigned, to redesign the destiny of my children to tradition of failure and late progress, die, in the name of Jesus.
34. Any ancestral bondage presently operating in the lives of my children, break by fire, in the name of Jesus.
35. Lord Jesus, fill the heart of my children with love and fear of God, in the name of Jesus.
36. Every arrow of affliction, fashioned against the destiny of my children, backfire, in the name of Jesus.
37. Every power jingling the bell of death on the destiny of my children, you and your evil bell die now in the name of Jesus.
38. Any power using my children's life to renew his life, I sentence you to sudden and untimely death, die, in the name of Jesus.
39. O Lord, disorganize all satanic decision taken at evil witchcraft coven, concerning the destiny of my children and let their evil plans backfire, in the name of Jesus.
40. Begin to thank the Lord for the deliverance of your children.

26. THE STORY OF MY CHILDREN WILL CHANGE

Praise Worship

Bible Passage -- Dan. 2:20-21, I Chron. 4:9-10

Confession: II Cor. 3:8

PRAYER POINTS

1. Lord Jesus, the lives of my children demand divine change, let their change come now by fire by force, in the name of Jesus.

2. O Lord, connect my children to your agenda for their lives, give them their desired change, that will make their case a miracle and a testimony, in the name of Jesus.

3. By the ordinances of God that ruleth the day and the night, I command every patterns of slavery and evil portion in the destiny of my children, break by fire and change for the best, in the name of Jesus.

4. Every satanic embargo and yoke of stagnation, assigned by evil powers of the father's house, to prevent my children from possessing their key of change, break by fire, in the name of Jesus.

5. O Lord, locate my children with unusual miracle of come and see that will completely change the story of their lives, in the name of Jesus.

6. Lord Jesus, give my children unexplainable progress in all areas of their endeavours, that will make them a name and a praise in their family line, in the name of Jesus.

7. By the power that divided the Red Sea and made a way where there is no way. O Lord, open unusual doors of prosperity for my children, that will make them become attraction, in the name Jesus.

8. Just as Lazarus was changed from a victim to a victor, from shame to fame, from mourning to dancing, O God, let the story of my children to a change for good, in the name Jesus.

9. Lord Jesus, You are the Unchanging Changer, promote divine possibilities in the lives of my children, that will change their story and make the world to notice them and celebrate with them, in the name of Jesus.

10. O God my Father, speak solution to the marital problems of my children and let their marital status change for good this year, in the name Jesus.

11. O Lord, restore the glory and the dignity of my children and let their career status change for better, in the name Jesus.

12. Lord Jesus, promote the business and labour of my children and let their financial status change tremendously, in the name Jesus.

13. O Lord, connect my daughter's to their rightful partners, so that their names, their habitation and their story may change for good, in the name Jesus.

14. By Your supernatural power, O Lord, change the barren situation of my children to fruitfulness and make them become proud parents of their children, in the name Jesus.

15. The power that changed the story of Jabez, from "Nobody" to become the most prominent among his family line, fall upon my children and let their story change, in the name Jesus.

16. The power that moved Joseph from prison to become Prime Minister in Egypt, promote the destiny of my children and let their story change, in the name Jesus.

17. My Father, remember all Your long expected promises in the lives of my children, let them come into fulfillment and change their story, in the name Jesus.

18. The miracle that the lives of my children have been waiting for, that will change their story and announce their names to the world, where ever you are now, appear, in the name Jesus.

19. Every long time problems, standing as mountain between my children and their breakthroughs, crumble and let my children enter into their season of change, in the name Jesus.

20. In this year, O Lord, arise and give my children a wonderful unexpected and unbelievable present, in the name of Jesus.

21. As the Three Wise Men presented baby Jesus with the most valuable and remarkable gifts, O Lord direct men and women to compete to bless my children with choicest gift, in the name Jesus.

22. My Father, give my children a reason to celebrate and be celebrated this year, in the name Jesus.

23. Begin to thank God for answer prayers.

OH GOD, GIVE MY CHILDREN NEW SONG

Praise Worship

Bible Passage: Psalm 40:1-5, Ps. 96:1-9, Ps. 98:1-9, Ps. 149, Ps. 33:3-12, Isaiah 42:10-17

Confession: Psalm 40:3

PRAYER POINTS

1. Oh Lord, let the voice of rejoicing and salvation continually be heard in the tabernacle of my children, in Jesus' name (Ps. 118:5)

2. Before the end of this year, O Lord, put joy in the heart of my children and laughter in their mouth that will provoke a new song, in the name Jesus.

3. Father Lord, remove the legs of my children from all ungodly journeys and remove their steps from every satanic diversion, in the name Jesus.

4. Every power from the father's house that needs to die for my children to sing a new song, your time is up, die, in the name Jesus.

5. Whether the enemy likes it or not, this month is your month of new song, begin to sing for joy, in the name Jesus.

6. Every enemy of joy, preventing my children, from singing a new song unto the Lord, you time is up, die, in the name Jesus.

7. O Lord, put a new song of victory, prosperity and advancement in the mouth of my children, in the name Jesus.

8. O God my Father, give key of outstanding, success and uncommon achievement to my children that will make them sing a new song this year, in the name Jesus.

9. My Father, restore the captivity of my children in a miraculous way give them a new name and let their mouth sing a new song, in the name Jesus.

10. O Lord, confuse the enemies of my children and make their enemies stepping stones for their advancement in life, in the name Jesus.

11. O Lord, do the unusual and the unexpected in the lives of my children that will make them breakforth into joy and sing a new song, in the name Jesus.

12. Every herbalist in possession of the name, picture, hair and clothe of my children, in order to do them evil, I command your evil work to backfire, in the name Jesus.

13. Every seed of witchcraft in the family of my children, withholding their season of joy, receive the thunder of fire of God and die, in the name Jesus.

14. I invoke the wrath of God on all household witchcraft and household wickedness, delaying my children's day of joy and new song, in the name of Jesus.

15. Every satanic prophesy, from any demonic church by any false prophet, in order to make witchcraft exchange of the virtues of my children, I cancel it with the blood of Jesus, in the name Jesus.

16. Every snake of darkness assigned to swallow the testimony of new song in the lives of my children, I chase you back to your sender, in the name Jesus.

17. Every fetish, ritual and sacrifice fashioned against the lives of my children, be frustrated, be disgraced and destroy your owner, in the name Jesus.

18. I prophesy into the lives of my children, that they will not rejoice in bondage, drink water of affliction or eat the bread of sorrow, in the name Jesus.

19. You my children, I decree into your lives that you will not live in shame, die in shame and be numbered among the wasted, in the name Jesus.

20. My father, according to your promise in Psalm 102:13, I declare that it is time for my children to sing a new song, in Jesus' name.

21. Every evil mark of hatred, rejection and failure in the lives of my children, preventing them from singing a new song, Blood of Jesus, rob them off and set them free, in the name Jesus.

22. Father Lord, by the power of your change, let the Marrah of my children receive sweetness, their Jericho demolished, closed doors opened to signs and wonders, and every impossible situation become divine possibility, in the name Jesus.

23. O Lord, send divine plagues upon the personal Pharaoh of my children, bring them to subjection and disgrace their pride, in the name Jesus.

24. Every bondage situation in the lives of my children, break and every power holding them captive, release them and die, in the name Jesus.

25. After the order of Mordeccai, O Lord, cause an event to happen that will promote my children into a testimony of new song, in the name Jesus.

26. O Lord, let new wells spring up in the desert of my children and let divine harvest, meet harvest in their lives, in the name Jesus.

27. O Lord, sort my children out and pick them out of the crowd for special blessing this year, in the name Jesus.

28. O Lord, let the divine seed in the lives of my children prosper like a palm tree, in the name Jesus.

29. Begin to thank God for answered prayers.

28 OH LORD, ANOINT MY CHILDREN FOR INCREASE

Praise Worship

Scripture Reading: Psalm 115:1 – 14

Confession: Psalm 71:21

PRAYER POINTS

1. Anointing for supernatural increase and greatness fall upon children this year, in the name of Jesus.

2. Every evil power and evil transaction, currently resisting increase and greatness in the life of my children, die, in the name of Jesus.

3. O God of promotion, increase the beneficial potentials of my children to excellence, in all areas of their lives, in the name of Jesus.

4. Any evil programme positioned into the career, marriage, conception, business, project and ministry of my children to hinder their increase, be dismantled, in the name of Jesus.

5. Every foundational bondage, connecting my children to internal and external demotion and stagnation, be consumed by Holy Ghost fire, in the name of Jesus.

6. Curse and covenant of limitation, working against the increase and greatness of my children, break by fire and let their heavens open, in the name of Jesus.

7. Spirit of reduction, assigned to destroy the anointing of increase upon the lives of my children, die, in the name of Jesus.

8. Strangers in close places, from the family line of my children, delegated to steal their key of increase, die, in the name of Jesus.

9. You my children, wherever you are, hear the word of the Lord, receive your key of increase to enlarge your coasts, in the name of Jesus.

10. O Lord, let your power of multiplication, increase my children more and more until their cup of progress is running over, in the name of Jesus.

11. Lord Jesus, increase Your wisdom, knowledge and understanding in the lives of my children until their lives will experience the excellent spirit, in the name of Jesus.

12. O Lord my God, let there be a daily increase in the joy of my children, until their joy is full and complete, in the name of Jesus.

13. According to Your Word, O Lord comfort my children on all sides and increase their greatness, in the name of Jesus.

14. Holy Spirit, decrease the works of the flesh and make the fruit of the spirit increase in the lives of my children, in the name of Jesus.

15. O Lord, water the garden of my children and let their barren land bring forth harvest of increase, in the name of Jesus.

16. My Father, let the spirit of giving, fall upon my children so that as they scatter, heavens will increase them, in the name of Jesus.

17. Lord Jesus, let my children increase in well doing, so that they can reap rich harvest of heavenly blessings, in the name of Jesus.

18. No matter what my children have lost to spiritual robbers, O Lord restore their captivity and let their latter end be greatly increased like job, in the name of Jesus.

19. Every Saul, pursuing the David of my children, in order to make them wandering star and hinder their increase, die, in the name of Jesus.

20. Every King Uzziah, reigning in the throne of my children to reduce their potentials for physical and spiritual increase, die, in the name of Jesus.

21. Every power mocking the Elisha of my children because of the "BUT" in their lives, die suddenly, in the name of Jesus.

22. Every curse and suffering of the Bible, pursue the enemies of increase in the lives of my children, in the name of Jesus.

23. Every power, gathered to mock and reproach my children because of their situation, receive open and double disgrace, in the name of Jesus.

24. Holy Spirit, increase Your fire, Your power and Your anointing in lives of my children for spiritual growth, in the name of Jesus.

25. O Lord, let Your beauty and Your glory be seen in the lives of my children everyday of their lives, in the name of Jesus.

26. O Lord my Father, let my children increase in wisdom and stature and in favour with God and man, in the name of Jesus.

27. Lord, Jesus, let the mantle of Elijah fall upon my children for double portion anointing and increased spiritual growth, in the name of Jesus.

28. You my children, I prophesy into your lives that you will not forsake me but you will remember me and take good care of me, in the name of Jesus.

29. Every invisible satanic remote control, targeted against the progress of my children, catch fire, in the name of Jesus.

30. Begin to thank God for answered prayers.

THE HOUR OF FAVOUR FOR MY CHILDREN HAS COME

Praise Worship

Scripture Reading: Gen. 39:13-23

Confession: Psalm 102:13

PRAYER POINTS

1. Lord Jesus, as Esther received uncommon favour from the king, let my children continue to grow in grace increase in favour with God and all the people, in the name of Jesus.

2. After the order of Joseph, O Lord, deliver my children from all the afflictions of their father's house and let Your favour catapult them to the exalted position that no one has ever attained in their family line, in the name of Jesus.

3. It does not matter whether my children desire it or not, they must receive unquantifiable favour from the Lord, to prevail with man and with God, in the name of Jesus.

4. O Lord, let my children find favour, compassion and loving kindness concerning their business, marriage, promotion, employment, proposals and give them supernatural breakthrough, in the name of Jesus.

5. My Father, let every demonic obstacles that has been established in the heart of _____ against favour for my children, be destroyed by fire, in the name of Jesus.

6. Favour of God, favour from God, overshadow my children make their lives bundles of testimonies and let their hour of celebration and jubilation manifest, in the name of Jesus.

7. O Lord, anoint my children with Your holy oil of favour for divine acceptance and approval before those who will help them, and break every yoke of delay and denials, in the name of Jesus.

8. My Father, put Your mark of favour upon my children and count them worthy among the few to be chosen for promotion, marriage, employment and admission, in the name of Jesus.

9. Lord Jesus, deposit magnet of favour in the lives of my children, that will link them with divine helpers and attract them to good and helpful people, in the name of Jesus.

10. By Your favour, O Lord, let a great and effectual door of breakthroughs that my children knock, open to them by their own accord before the end of this year, in the name of Jesus.

11. My Father, soak the lives of my children with Your favour and let their lives attract the favour of God and man, everywhere they go for help, in the name of Jesus.

12. Father Lord, release Your favour, as dew of heaven upon every dry bone situation, in the lives of my children to come alive, in the name of Jesus. (Prov. 19:21)

13. O Lord my Father, let the horns of my children be exalted and let Your favour continually meet favour in their lives, in the name of Jesus.

14. O Lord, let Your favour upon my children be their mark of distinction and let every mark of hatred, jealousy and envy, working against favour and limiting their goodness, be erased by the blood of Jesus, in the name of Jesus.[

15. Sing this song "Let God Arise ---" three times, then pray this prayer.

    O God, arise in all Your power and destroy anything working against favour in the lives of my children, in the name of Jesus.

16. My Father, let favour speak for my children and let the peace, joy good health, job, promotion, pregnancy, marriage and material assets they have lost, be restored to them, in the name of Jesus.

17. Every stronghold of household witchcraft and household wickedness, working together against divine favour for my children, thunder fire of God, comfound their language and destroy them, in the name of Jesus.

18. Every power from the grave, water, sky, mountain, forest underneath the earth, working against goodness and favour in the lives of my children, perish by fire, in the name of Jesus.

19. Abraham received favour, Daniel received favour, Mary received favour, Joseph received favour, Esther received favour, therefore, the case of my children must not be different. O Lord favour my children, in the name of Jesus.

20. Favour, favour, favour, wherever you are, the lives of my children are available for you, enter, in the name of Jesus.

21. O God, as You turned again the captivity of Zion, let my children receive favour for divine restoration and turn-around breakthroughs, in the name of Jesus.

22. My Father and my God, let my children receive Angelic visitation of favour after the order of Peter and be delivered from the prison house of the enemy, waiting to disgrace their God, in the name of Jesus.

ANOINTED DESTINY CHANGING PRAYERS FOR YOUR CHILDREN

23. Lord Jesus, put the garment of favour upon my children and let garment of disgrace and reproach upon them, catch fire and burn to ashes, in the name of Jesus.

24. My Father, let Your favour open book of remembrance for my children, after the order of Mordeccai, and let their wicked foes be the ones that will usher them into their place of special honour, in the name of Jesus.

25. The grace that produces unmerited favour, locate my children, Trinity of goodness, mercy and favour, make their lives, your permanent abode, in the name of Jesus.

26. O Lord, baptize my children with Spirit of favour, let Your mercy provoke favour in their lives and bring them into favour with the helpers that will promote their destiny, in the name of Jesus.

27. Every witchcraft covenant of no favour made by the powers of the Father's house of my children, and every ritual and sacrifice prepared against favour for them, I reverse it by the blood of Jesus, backfire and work against your owner, in the name of Jesus.

28. Father Lord, let the wind of favour from four corners of the world blow to my children, open a way for them where there is no way, and let people compete to help and bless them, in the name of Jesus.

29. Sign this song seven (7) times as you wave the photographs of your children to heavens.

    I can see everything turning around in their favour.

30. Begin to thank God for answered prayers.

30 MERCY OF GOD, SPEAK FOR MY CHILDREN

Praise Worship

Scripture Reading: Psalm 136 (Responsively)

Confession: Psalm 103:17

PRAYER POINTS

1. Sing the song: Thy mercy always do I seek O God

   As you sing the chorus, wave photographs to heaven.

1. Thy mercy always do I seek O God,
   Send Thy mercy to us; (for my children)
   Birds in the air and ants that on the earth,
   Do receive Thy mercy.

   Mercy, mercy, mercy, mercy,
   Thy mercy heavenly father;
   I am pleading for; (for my children)
   Birds in the air and ants that on the earth,
   Do receive Thy mercy.

2. Mercy just like that of blind Bartimaeu,
   I am seeking from Thee; (for my children)
   That all who are invalid among us,
   May receive Thy mercy.

3. Esther the old Queen never forgot Thee,
   In her time of trouble;
   She conquered all her enemies with prayer
   God Thou defendeth her.

4. David would never forget Thy mercy,
   Before great Goliath;
   Daniel also in the den of lions,
   Has Thee as his shelter.

5. The sun shines in the day by Thy power,
   So the moon in the night;
   The wet and the dry season in the year,
   Are all in Thy own hands.

6. Let people show mercy to my children,
   In miraculous ways
   Let divine helps rise up for their sake
   By Your loving mercy.

2. O God of mercy, plead the cause of my children anywhere they carried their names or matter, to do them evil, and make evil to befall them, in the name of Jesus.

3. I bring my children to the altar of mercy and before the mercy seat, my Father, arise and show them your great mercy, in the name of Jesus.

4. As You showed great mercy unto David, O Lord, grant my children the greatest of Your mercy in the sight of those who will help them, in the name of Jesus.

5. Anywhere and everywhere my children go, compass them about with the multitude of Your mercy and open doors of turn-around breakthrough for them, in the name of Jesus.

6. Unto You O Lord belongeth mercy and You are plenteous in mercy to all. The lives of my children are waiting for the manifestation of Your great mercy, appear, in the name of Jesus.

7. O Lord, let Your mercy reveal to my children the beneficial potentials of their lives that will push them into the mountain of prosperity, in the name of Jesus.

8. After the order of Blind Bartemeous, I cry unto You for my children, My father, have mercy on them and help them, in the name of Jesus.

9. By your mercy O Lord, let rivers of divine helps flow into the lives of my children and sink every hopeless and helpless situation in their lives, in the name of Jesus.

10. Every problem that is mocking prayer and making God a liar in the lives of my children, in Your mercy O Lord, deliver them, in the name of Jesus.

11. Before the end of this year, O Lord, arise suddenly with Your mercy, surprise my children with a miracle that will make them to be celebrated, in the name of Jesus.

12. Mercy of God, speak for my children, close every road of backwardness and loose open heavens, new open doors and new opportunities for them in the name of Jesus.

13. Great mercy of God, speak for my children at the altar of mercy, promote them and let their story change, in the name of Jesus.

14. Mercy of God, Favour of God, Grace of God, Glory of God, Blessing of God, work together for my children and promote their destiny, in the name of Jesus.

15. My Father, Your slogan for my children this year is Mercy and Unprecedented Favour. Let this be their testimony this year, in the name of Jesus.

16. Lord Jesus, make my children vessels of Your mercy and overshadow them with Your surplus mercy, in the name of Jesus.

17. Mercy of God, Blood of Jesus, Name of Jesus, speak for my children, in the name of Jesus.

18. In line with Lamentation 3:23, O Lord, renew Your mercy upon my children and bath them with fresh mercy and favour, in the name of Jesus.

19. O Lord, by Your mercy and power, prosper whatever my children lay their hands upon to do and restore whatever was lost in their lives, in the name of Jesus.

20. God of mercy, who is rich and plenteous in mercy, my children need Your mercy, arise in Your mercy and let mercy speak for them, at the altar of mercy, so that:

(a) those seeking for job will find favour and get a good job that will make them happy and comfortable in life.

(b) those praying for the fruit of the womb will become pregnant, carry the pregnancy to full time and be safely delivered.

(c) those who are yet single will be divinely magnetized to their rightful partner and be happily married.

(d) those whose promotions have been delayed or denied, will receive their letters of promotion to the next level.

(e) those who want to further their education, helpers will arise for them and they will get admission with ease.

(f) those who have uncompleted projects will receive anointing of Zerubbabel and complete them with ease and comfort.

(g) dry bone situation in any area of their lives with receive resurrection power of Jesus and come alive.

21. Sing this song as you wave the photographs of your children to heaven.

Surely, goodness and mercy, shall follow them
All the days, all the days of my children. } 2ce

22. Begin to thank God for answered prayers.